The Little
Black Book of
Business
Meetings

The Little
Black Book of
Business
Meetings

Michael C. Thomsett

amacom
American Management Association

This book is available at a special
discount when ordered in bulk quantities.
For information, contact Special Sales Department,
AMACOM, a division of American Management Association,
135 West 50th Street, New York, NY 10020.

Library of Congress Cataloging-in-Publication Data

Thomsett, Michael C.
   The little black book of business meetings / Michael C. Thomsett.
      p.   cm.
   ISBN 0-8144-7716-X
   1. Meetings.   2. Business communication.   I. Title.
   HF5733.5.T48   1989
   658.4'56—dc20   89-45458
                                                            CIP

Printing number

10 9 8 7 6 5 4 3 2 1

Contents

Introduction

Outside of traffic, there is nothing that has held this country back as much as committees.

—Will Rogers

If you have been involved with the business world for more than a few days, you already know that communication determines how well we work with one another. The daily task of explaining, updating, advising, and consulting within an organization occurs verbally, through memoranda, and in the business meeting.

So concerned is management with the creation of a working communications system that meetings often become the primary forum for airing points of view. This "corporate social action" often involves many dimensions of interaction and presents the opportunity to encourage and build worthwhile communication.

This Little Black Book examines the opportunities, problems, and unspoken cultural rules involved in the internal meeting. The book is informally divided into two sections, which occasionally overlap. In the first section, which encompasses Chapters 1 through 6, we will basically be concerned with leading meetings, with the goal of showing how the best results can be achieved, how the needs of attendees can be met through fair and balanced leadership, and how the successful actions defined by the meeting are brought together with follow-up.

The second section of the book—the last six chapters—explains the intricacies of participation, generally from the point of view of the meeting attendee. This applies to departmental status meetings, decision-making and policy-setting meetings, or purely informational gatherings.

The meetings you lead or attend can either serve a valuable purpose in your career and in the priorities you face each day, or they can become a time-consuming waste of effort. The effectiveness of meetings in every organization depends on the attitudes and actions of participants. You can make a difference by setting a positive tone for meetings and defining what they must achieve.

We will propose a number of action steps for the preparation and control of agendas, the number of people invited to attend, and the all-important steps that must occur *after* the meeting. All of these issues are explained with the use of examples, and every chapter concludes with work projects. Solutions to these, as well as additional ideas, are given in the appendix at the back of the book.

Many theories postulate how best to prepare and control meetings in the corporation. However, the day-to-day realities you face differ from textbook descriptions, because real meetings are staffed with real people. Every meeting therefore involves an element of suspense. Every attendee in every meeting has an agenda, which is not necessarily the same agenda you have before you.

This Little Black Book is your personal reference for attending and running successful meetings. With this book, you will be able to propose methods for improving your organization's meetings—saving time, doing away with waste, and creating a forum for truly effective modes of communication leading to action and success. However, this book should be kept under lock and key somewhere in your desk. Do *not* take it to meetings. Many cases have been reported in which copies of this book disappeared mysteriously during the shuffling of paperwork. Protect your investment as a personal career trade secret.

1

Your Internal Forum

There is no such thing as a worthless conversation, provided you know what to listen for.

—James Nathan Miller

The president of the company wrote a memo to all managers and executives, instructing that the number of meetings must be cut by one-half. One vice-president went to the president's office, memo in hand, and asked, "When was this decided?" The president said that the decision was made during a meeting of the finance committee. The vice-president asked, "Why wasn't I invited?"

You have been given a challenging assignment: to plan and organize a weekly meeting, including making assignments and following up with those in attendance. From a subordinate's point of view, this may represent the ultimate achievement: power, prestige, and influence, and all of that in a comfortable boardroom chair, while the troops remain back in the department, doing the actual work.

An employee who has never run a meeting and, perhaps, attended only a few if any, might envy the manager or executive who attains such a high degree of status that the job itself includes going to meetings. That's where the decisions are made, where directions are forged, and where middle managers make names for themselves and begin their climb to the top—or so goes the myth.

The truth is far removed from this glamorous idea of what goes on behind that conference room door. In fact, meetings are hard work, sensitive and highly charged, and complex in both work and cultural demands. A properly planned meeting can be your forum for influencing the quality of product or service, for saving money and creating future profits, and for improving communication between departments. Going to a meeting can be the best investment of your management time.

Anyone who attends a large number of meetings knows that they can be tedious and unstimulating if they are not well led and well planned. A job that consisted solely of meeting attendance—without the chance to do anything else—would be a most unrewarding form of work. And yet many managers and executives do spend too much of their time meeting with others, without gaining a constructive result. You can make the meetings you attend worth the time and effort by ensuring that they are work sessions, and not just sessions that take you away from work. A worthwhile meeting, far from being tedious, can help you to achieve the objectives of your job and of your department.

THE PURPOSE OF MEETINGS

A meeting is worthwhile *only* when it enables you and your organization to achieve positive, tangible results. That doesn't mean that, in the opinion of management, a meeting proves its worth by improving communication, which is intangible and subjective. If positive results are to be expected, they must be measurable and tangible. When they can be achieved without a formal meeting, then the meeting should never be held.

A meeting should contain several attributes, each designed to ensure that the leader and the attendees do benefit and do make good use of their time together. This demands adequate advance planning, both of materials and topics; the participation of everyone who does attend; and a concrete, measurable result.

Employees do not want to spend two or three hours in a meeting room, listening to discussions of little or no concern to them or to their departments. Nor do they want to walk away from a meeting with that nagging feeling that they did not make a contribution.

Most of us desire the opposite. We want to be included in a lively discussion with other creative and motivated managers, all interested in achieving a result. That doesn't mean that meetings require consensus; in fact, some of the most dynamic results develop from heated debate and constructive disagreement. And at the close of a meeting, there is nothing quite as satisfying as knowing that you contributed an idea, offered an observation, or arrived at a solution that solved the problem at hand.

Participation—not attendance alone, but real, active participation— requires that you enter the meeting room with a full understanding of the meeting's purpose and objectives. Depending on the type of meeting, this might be to get or give information, to learn something, to set a policy, or to make a decision. In most instances a meeting will demand some form of follow-up action. Thus, a good starting point is to attend with one critical question in mind: *What action must be taken, by whom, and when, to solve the problem?*

This will not apply, of course, when a meeting is held just to convey information or to provide training. But most meetings attended by managers involve a series of related problems, are held on a recurring basis, and include those people who are in a position to work toward a constructive solution (or at the very least, who will be affected by the decisions that are made).

A well-structured meeting contains these attributes (see Figure 1-1):

1. *Limited participation.* All of those in attendance are essential to the agenda. Whenever your meetings include people who do not *need* to be there, your problems begin.

2. *Specific agenda.* The meeting should be organized along the lines of an agenda that lists a limited number of subjects to be discussed and resolved. A general discussion only means that more time is required and less action results.

3. *Time limits.* Meetings should always start on time and should be identified by length. When the time is up, the meeting should end. This limit helps all participants to plan and stay within the confines of the agenda.

Figure 1-1. Attributes of meetings.

1. Limited participation

2. Specific agenda

3. Time limits

4. Control

5. Alternatives

6. Follow-up

4. *Control.* As positive as the idea of participation is, it has its limits. Yes, the attendees at a meeting should contribute something of value. But no, the meeting cannot be a completely democratic process. One person must be in control. This is not to say that attendees should sit quietly while that person does all of the speaking. That's not a meeting. It does mean that the form of participation practiced in the meeting is moderated by the organizer.

5. *Alternatives.* The greatest benefit of a meeting must be that solutions may come from anyone. If attendees are allowed to propose solutions to problems, chances are the best answer will come from the meeting—where it might not be possible in isolation.

Everyone has a point of view and a frame of reference. A difficult problem is best addressed when many points of view are considered, which, in turn, is worth something only if ideas can be acted on and problems solved.

6. *Follow-up.* A meeting is worthwhile only if decisions are made that would not be possible without the meeting, and then only if some form of appropriate action is taken. It is not enough for everyone to

agree on what *should* be done. Someone must assume specific responsibility for follow-up.

IDENTIFYING THE MEETING

Proper preparation can begin only when you understand the type of meeting you will lead or attend. The purpose, format, and attendance all dictate the nature of a meeting.

Categories of meetings include the following (see Figure 1-2):

1. *Information meetings.* Your chance to participate will be minimal when the meeting's purpose is solely to inform. Some meetings are called to make announcements about promotions or explain policy decisions, for example.

This type of meeting can involve receiving or giving information,

Figure 1-2. Meeting categories.

1. Information

2. Problem–solving

3. Creative

4. Policy

5. Training

6. Recurring task

7. General

or both. When you call a meeting to ask for information from others, preplanning must include giving attendees adequate preparation time. And by the same argument, you can best participate as an attendee when you know well in advance what information the meeting organizer wants to find.

2. *Problem-solving meetings.* This form of meeting, one of the most common, might also be called a decision-making meeting. The relationship between solving problems and making decisions is an important one. They go together. No problem is truly solved only by discussion; a decision must be made and followed through so that the solution can become a reality.

3. *Creative meetings.* The brainstorming session can be one of the most enjoyable forms of meeting. It allows you the chance to think aloud with others, to combine partial ideas into tangible avenues for new ideas, products, or services; marketing strategies; and any number of other solutions. Not every brainstorming session will result in solutions, and a creative meeting can easily become an unproductive exercise. But if proper guidelines are provided by a meeting leader, a limited number of creative sessions can be as valuable as a more tangible problem-solving meeting.

4. *Policy meeting.* Some meetings are called to solve a specific problem not by operational actions, but by the establishment of new policies. Creating the proper policy might require a great deal of discussion to arrive at what might seem a relatively small result. But a policy that affects a large number of departments cannot be established in isolation.

5. *Training meetings.* In many environments the need for continuing orientation and training demands that a series of meetings must be conducted. For example, companies that recruit new salespeople each month must ensure that the new members of the team thoroughly understand the product the company offers to the market. A training meeting must have a carefully organized and well-planned agenda, with each element carefully timed and scheduled. This is modified as new training material is added, or as better delivery methods are discovered.

6. *Recurring task meetings.* The most productive form of meeting should include a limited number of people and should exist only when

its value is proved over a period of time. Nowhere is this more true than in the recurring meeting. It might be called a "task force," a "review," a "status meeting," or an "update." The approach is worthwhile when a few managers or employees meet weekly, for example, with a supervisor or executive, to introduce new ideas, report the status of ongoing projects, or examine solutions to problems they share.

The task force idea is effective as long as it is held in check—in terms of both the number of people in attendance and the length of the meeting itself. One pitfall in this type of meeting is that, once its effectiveness is realized, more attendees are added, and the agenda is expanded. However, you must remember that this meeting is valuable only *because* it involves a few people and takes little time. Once these attributes change, the value of the meeting will decline.

7. *The general meeting.* An executive may call any number of managers together, either on a regular basis or as the need demands. The purpose of the general meeting is to bring up and, hopefully, to resolve a number of agenda subjects.

Common problems of general meetings include the attendance issue. Too many people, most of whom have little direct interest in most of the agenda, make for an ineffective, time-wasting meeting. Even with the best-prepared agenda, general meetings tend to be the least efficient.

A specific agenda, advance planning, time limits, and firm leadership will help make a periodic general meeting a more positive and constructive experience. As long as required actions are identified, assigned, given a deadline, and followed up, the general meeting improves communication between departments and individuals and helps create a sense of real teamwork.

If you are expected to act as a meeting leader, call meetings that involve as few people as possible, and then build a specific agenda around those people and their common concerns. For example, within one section, three or four departments might participate in a recurring monthly meeting to plan a monthly closing routine. This situation might require only a short gathering, simply to coordinate and time the team effort.

Example: In one service organization, the chief accountant called monthly meetings for managers of three different accounting departments under his control. The declared purpose of the meeting was to coordinate efforts for month-end closing. However, the meetings consisted of the chief accountant asking, "Does anyone have any problems to bring up?" followed by a general silence, with each attendee waiting for someone else to speak. Then the chief accountant would conclude with a statement like "It's going to be a tough closing this month" or "Let's all be sure to work together."

These brief, pointless meetings were the subject of many jokes. Obviously, the chief accountant understood the importance of getting his team together, but knew nothing about what should be discussed at those meetings. The reasons for this problem included:

1. *No agenda.* The "agenda" was a vague requirement that somehow the managers must work together. Problems in past months were not raised and resolved, specific difficulties in the current month were not confronted, and the managers were given nothing to react to. The meeting had no focus.

2. *No goals.* The chief accountant failed to vocally identify specific goals for the group. Thus, there could be no teamwork; there was no indication of what the group hoped to achieve.

3. *No participation.* Imagine how productive these meetings could have been if the chief accountant had started out by asking each attendee, "From your point of view, what problems did we encounter at last month's closing? How can we avoid the same problems this month?" No participation occurred because none was invited. It's an unavoidable fact of business life that people will rarely offer to speak even though they may speak well when asked. A poor leader is mystified that no one speaks up at his meetings, but a good leader knows the importance of allowing attendees to contribute their ideas.

MYTHS ABOUT PARTICIPATION

What does "participative management" really mean? This admirable idea has become a buzzword for many things and, unfortunately, the original concept is poorly understood by a number of corporate managers and employees.

To some, "participation" means remembering everyone's name, specific job description, or previous employers. To others, it means gathering *numbers* of people together. The more people in a meeting, the greater the participation. More voices mean more ideas, more and better solutions, and improved morale. This theory also embraces the idea that employees will always remain happy as long as they think they're being given the chance to participate.

In fact, participation must be backed with much more than a handshake and first-name recognition. Real participation means that you are given the chance to voice an opinion, influence the outcome of a discussion, and be directly involved in a solution. Several myths prevail about the value and significance of participation in meetings, including:

Myth Number 1: The more people on the team, the better the team. The reality is that smaller groups are more efficient, and they work better than a large committee. It's easier to assign responsibility for action, to follow up and judge results, and to get things done. The larger the group, the greater the tendency to avoid taking action, to speak in generalities, and to fail in the important follow-up actions that decisions demand.

Myth Number 2: Holding a lot of meetings means communication will improve. The unfortunate fact is, when a lot of people go to a lot of meetings, their communication level falls off, and so does their productivity. Communication works only if it produces results and solves problems. As long as you're sitting in a meeting, you can't solve problems under discussion. You can decide how to solve them and accept the assignment, but the real work must take place back in your department.

Myth Number 3: All you need to do is get people together and raise questions. The answers will come from interaction. Solutions must come from hard work, making difficult decisions based on research and facts, and respecting other people's points of view. No organization can solve its problems just by calling meetings. Discussion is a useful exercise as long as action results. But merely talking about a problem does not mean a solution will be found, or that follow-up will occur.

Myth Number 4: Taking action is the leader's role. Thus, the meeting's leader must ultimately be responsible for all follow-up action. This common belief is used to avoid taking responsibility for following up. But a meeting is only as good as the collective commitment its participants are willing and able to make. The leader may assume the role of ensuring that follow-up occurs. And the leader might be the one who asks for action from one or more of the others in attendance. But if all attendees believe they do not have to do any of the work, why are they attending the meeting?

Myth Number 5: Meetings are valuable because they clear the air and result in consensus. Differences of opinion may be expressed at meetings, and a final decision may be made. But that does not mean that everyone leaves a meeting in complete accord. Chances are, opposing points of view will only be strengthened as a result of meetings. Some managers believe that a meeting clears the air; it's more likely that each person attending will come away with his or her own conclusions about what was achieved, what was decided, and what follow-up actions will be taken. That's why great care must be taken to ensure that all attendees know what was decided at the meeting—even if they were there.

Myth Number 6: As long as everyone has the chance to express a point of view, the meeting will be a success. A successful meeting cannot be determined by the level of discussion. Some of the most "interactive" meetings may achieve the least. Freedom of expression is of little value in an organization, except to the extent that it leads to solutions. A successful meeting takes place only when individuals respond to the discussion by taking actions that solve problems.

See Figure 1-3 for a summary of these meeting myths versus the realities.

USING MEETINGS PROPERLY

The number of meetings held in your company should not be the test of communication, nor of effectiveness in getting work done. Frequent meetings may be a sign of inaction rather than an indication that any real

Figure 1-3. Common myths.

MYTH	REALITY
The number of attendees defines a quality team.	Smaller groups are more efficient.
Frequent meetings improve communication.	Communication is the product of action.
Interaction leads to solutions.	Solutions come from hard work.
Taking action is the leader's role.	Attendees are responsible for follow-up action.
Meetings lead to consensus.	People interpret meetings in different ways.
Free expression defines a successful meeting.	Discussion alone cannot lead to action.

progress is taking place. Remember that going to meetings means time away from your department; a meeting might be necessary to decide what must be done, but action occurs only when the meeting is over.

Example: The managers of every department spend between four and eight hours per week in participative team meetings. This task force is intended to address problems of concern to the entire organization. But while many problems are raised and discussed, the meetings do not lead to action. This is true because:

1. They take up too much time.
2. Too many people are involved.
3. Much of the discussion involves topics of interest to only a few of those in attendance.
4. Follow-up action is never identified, and no specific assignments are given out.

When top management calls a series of meetings to raise and discuss problems, but fails to insist on action, that is a sign of ineffective leadership. If the problems are truly of concern to a broad cross-section of the organization, then it must be management's task to solve them. And if the problems are specific to only one or two departments, meetings should be limited to those managers.

A successful meeting is one that succeeds according to the number of solutions generated. If you can point to meetings you attend or lead and identify tangible value that came from those meetings, then you're on the right track. Such meetings are typified by specific assignments, action, and review. They are *not* a waste of time; on the contrary, you cannot afford to pass up the chance to hold the most productive meeting, nor can you afford to miss the opportunity to identify action steps.

Many organizations hold truly effective meetings that result in solutions. But many others use the forum to debate issues and draw no conclusions. Even with the best of intentions, it sometimes proves difficult to make the transition between identifying problems and making the tough decisions that will resolve them.

If no one defines what actions should be taken, by whom, or by what deadline, you can be certain that the problem *will* come up again. There is no opportunity to review progress of the solution, because the consensus of the group was not to solve anything, but to go on to the next agenda item.

Meetings that do not lead to action harm morale and make all attendees less effective. Rather than achieving improved communication, managers find that even when the frequency of meetings is increased, results are as elusive as ever.

ADOPTING AN ACTION STRATEGY

Judging the value of meetings is fairly simple. If you can readily see the value of investing time, you are taking the right approach. But what if you believe that meetings are nothing more than a waste of time? How can you make a difference in this case?

Whether you lead a meeting or are one of several attendees, you can help improve the quality of meetings in your organization. We will make several assumptions to show how this can be done. First, let's assume that you have attended several meetings lately and that you are dissatisfied with the results. Nothing gets decided or done. No follow-up actions are specified. And no one clearly agrees on the issues at hand. We will also assume that the usual purpose of your meetings is to solve a specific problem. This is the most common form of meeting—to make a decision related to one problem or a range of problems.

As a leader or as an attendee, you have the opportunity to change the status quo. If meetings in your organization serve no real value, you can make a difference. You can be the one person who insists on results, by always asking four key questions (see Figure 1-4):

1. *Who is responsible for solving this problem?* Even when a problem is of concern to everyone in the room, a solution will be possible only when someone is given the primary job of executing it.

2. *How can the rest of us help?* If you're not willing to work with others in solving problems raised before the group, then you shouldn't be at the meeting. Add real meaning to the word "participation" by volunteering to work with others.

Figure 1-4. Four key questions.

```
1. Who is responsible for
   solving this problem?

2. How can the rest of
   us help?

3. What course of action
   should be taken?

4. What's the deadline?
```

3. *What course of action should be taken?* Agreeing that a solution is mandated is the first step. But the job really begins once a plan is developed. The solution can be put into action only if the plan first exists.

4. *What's the deadline?* Achievement can never be measured or judged without a timetable. Thus, the deadline is essential. Once it has been agreed on, it can be evaluated at the next month's meeting, and progress can be monitored.

Example: One manager went to each meeting with a list of the four key questions in front of him. He asked these questions each time an agenda item was raised. They always resulted in discussion and, ultimately, a decision that led to action. And if the questions were not answered because a discussion wandered into other areas, the manager repeated them.

After attending several meetings and using this technique, the manager saw a difference. The meetings he attended led to results. More than just a gathering of committees, they included agenda items that called for solutions.

Whether you participate as one of several managers or lead a meeting yourself, use these questions as your own guidelines. Only by insisting that they be addressed can you ensure that meetings will be worthwhile and productive.

CHARACTERISTICS OF MEETINGS

The four key questions will work in many different types of meetings. However, to plan your strategy for participation, you must also understand the purpose and nature of every meeting. A meeting can be defined in terms of the number of people in attendance, by topic, by frequency, by the composition of people, and by motivation.

The Number of People

Smaller meetings are more likely to produce results, because assignment responsibility is more easily identified. In a large group the issue of *who* should take action might never come up, especially when too much time and effort are spent debating departmental points of view.

Example: A meeting includes managers from every department in the company. Among the agenda items is a discussion of an unfavorable budget variance in your department. A lengthy discussion ensues, in which several other managers present their points of view on the problems of budgeting. After some time another topic is raised and your problem is passed over. However, two weeks later you meet with the vice-president and bring up the problem. During this discussion you develop a course of action to control expenses in your department and to avoid future overruns.

Topic

In an organization where communication is a real and tangible practice, every meeting is planned with a preliminary agenda. And every participant has the chance to comment before it is finalized. In this environment you also have enough influence to have items put onto an agenda or removed from it.

In the real world, however, this premise assumes a great deal. First, a good number of meetings are thrown together without an agenda in mind, written or otherwise. Second, when there is a written agenda, most attendees see it for the first time when they show up at the meeting. Thus, they have no opportunity to prepare for the discussion of any of the issues. And third, few people are given the chance to comment on what will be discussed at the meeting.

Frequency

Meetings can be defined by how often they occur. You might attend one-of-a-kind meetings or a series of recurring ones. We are concerned primarily with the latter type, since most companies organize a number of periodic meetings familiar to managers—budget review, departmental or project status, and monthly reporting meetings, for example.

Most of the problems you encounter as a meeting leader or attendee are also recurrent. Because they are familiar, their solutions can be studied and observed. You have the opportunity to experiment and can also gauge how far you have progressed as a meeting participant and what level of effectiveness you have achieved.

Composition

Who attends meetings? In some smaller companies a number of recurring meetings are attended by the entire staff. This is one of the potential advantages of the smaller organization: communication is made easier because everyone is accessible. In a larger organization the scope and number of people complicate the meeting problem and demand different solutions.

Example: One marketing firm had only five employees in its second year of operation. The firm contracted with a number of independent, self-employed sales offices in its territory and was able to manage the centralized office with little trouble. Weekly staff meetings helped everyone in the home office to communicate well and to act on projects and problems. However, as the company grew, so did the number of employees. The weekly meetings were abandoned as managers and executives were recruited. Unfortunately, the rank and file became more isolated from the decision-making process, and morale suffered as a result.

While top managers and executives probably need to meet on a more regular basis than do entry-level employees, there remains a need to keep all employees involved. The meeting forum can serve as an excellent method for achieving this desirable goal, if used properly.

Motivation

Why are meetings called? This question identifies meetings just as it predicts how well meeting time is used. As long as the meeting has a clear purpose and goal, and as long as the meeting is the most effective way to achieve that goal, meetings will be productive exercises in management. But if personal influence, politics, or passing the buck are the motives for holding meetings, their quality rapidly declines.

AN ACTION ORIENTATION

Most people agree that results are important. As a corporate employee, you know that success is invariably defined in terms of dollars and cents. The greater the profit from a decision, the better the decision. This is the standard for performance on every level in the organization. Management keeps track of its progress based on how today's profit results compare to last year's, to a forecast, and to the competition.

Even recognizing this reality, meetings become symbols of prestige and influence—regardless of how much benefit they actually produce. The idea is that important people must attend a large number of meetings, and attendance itself becomes a type of corporate status symbol. That creates a cycle that's difficult to break, just as it's difficult to get off the junk mail lists once your name and address are passed around.

Once an individual gets on the list and begins attending meetings, the influence and importance that seem to result cannot be ignored. Later, if that person's name is dropped from the list, he seems to lose influence and status. This is unfortunate, because merely attending a meeting is not a sign of importance. Rather, the judgment about a person's performance should be based on results he achieves. If you attend a large number of meetings and as a result are able to solve problems, then the meetings are worthwhile. If, on the other hand, you can function better without a large number of meetings, you are no less important than someone who spends virtually all his or her time in the conference room.

Meetings are important events in the corporate culture. The impression and image we hold in the organization are important and affect our morale and self-esteem. So while we need to try and control the time we spend away from our department, it is equally important to strive for validity when we are in meetings.

Example: You attend a meeting with a report in hand, proposing a major procedural change. You expect resistance, but have developed statistical proof that your idea will save the company a great deal of money each year. While other attendees admit that your idea has merit, they raise several issues you overlooked. A reevaluation leads to acceptance, but only in such a way that the needs and priorities in other departments are respected and acknowledged.

This is an example of how a meeting should always work. You might have a very specific point of view, which leads you to conclude that the "right" answer is obvious. But in a meeting setting, you come to understand that your point of view—as valid as it might be—cannot always take in the larger picture. A suggestion for a change, for example, might have ramifications for others of which you were unaware. So the best solution must often be modified so that everyone can endorse it.

How can you adopt an action motive? Follow these guidelines for every meeting you attend:

1. *What contributes to the problem?* Problems can be resolved only when you understand how they came about. Many problems can be temporarily solved, or solutions might have the appearance of finality. But in fact, the response might not do away with the problem. To make

your actions most effective, be sure you understand the nature of a problem.

2. *Always look to the long term.* Given the nature of meetings—with a number of voices contributing ideas and debating priorities—it's easy to forget about the future. Solutions may, in fact, represent short-term compromise. Improve your action orientation by always questioning how solution ideas might appear a year down the road.

3. *Look at issues from the other side.* You will be the most effective meeting participant when you're able to see a problem from the other person's point of view. For example, you propose a solution and another manager argues strongly against it. Before adopting a completely defensive stance, think about that other person's priorities. Chances are, your idea is threatening or unworkable. And the *next* time you propose a solution, you will be better prepared and able to devise a solution that's broader.

The action orientation that leads to productive and successful meetings is achieved both by leaders and attendees. We will address both points of view. In the next few chapters, the leader's role will be examined and explained. Chapter 2 shows how leaders can take an active part in creating a thriving meeting environment for their fellow employees.

WORK PROJECT

1. You have been attending a weekly meeting for several months. However, there is never an agenda or a time limit, and most attendees do not participate. What suggestions can you make to improve this meeting?

2. Identify three myths about meetings, and explain the realities. How can you apply these to meetings you attend in your company?

3. Name the four questions that should be addressed for every agenda item in every meeting. Explain how you can improve the quality of meetings by raising these questions.

2

Leading the Meeting: The Active Role

In a good meeting there is a momentum that comes from the spontaneous exchange of fresh ideas and produces extraordinary results. That momentum depends on the freedom permitted the participants.

—Harold Geneen

The accounting manager, while leading a budget review meeting, commented that the company needed yet another revision—the third in less than two months. As the attendees let out a collective groan, one sales rep at the far end of the conference table whispered something to the person next to him, who snickered in response.
"What was that?" the accounting manager growled.
The sales rep shot back, "I said, let's get a rope."

The leader sets the tone. A meeting can be either productive, dynamic, and progressive or a frustrating exercise in disorganization. It can allow others to voice ideas in a positive, nonthreatening environment, or it can be used to suppress ideas. And the leader can either firmly exert control over the agenda or allow the meeting to decline into a disorganized, directionless experience.

The leader may play many roles in conducting the meeting. Ensuring that all agenda items are covered within a limited amount of time is only the *obvious* service a leader provides. There's much more.

ACHIEVING DESIRED RESULTS

To be an effective, respected leader, you must have a clear focus on what your meeting should achieve. But in that context you must first determine whether the meeting is the best forum for your agenda. Then you must be prepared to control three phases of meeting management: advance planning, leading the meeting itself, and follow-up.

1. *Advance planning.* The steps you take before the meeting actually occurs will determine its effectiveness, to a large degree. Who should be there, how long should it take, and of course, what will be discussed? What people should you see before the meeting, so that they can prepare for any reports you will need, materials you'll need passed out, or important questions they will have to answer? And when will your agenda be published? Hopefully, you will have time to publish your agenda well in advance of the meeting, so that attendees will also be able to plan before the meeting itself.

2. *Leading the meeting.* How should you conduct yourself during the meeting? The best leadership might appear effortless to observers when, in fact, it requires experience and a sincere desire to lead well. Some managers are not aware of the need for keeping a balance between control and openness, and they mistakenly hold their meetings with an iron fist. Thus, no one contributes or even speaks up. Others prefer popularity to a closely controlled meeting and exercise no leadership at all. Somewhere in the middle is the relaxed, cordial, but controlled meeting—in which the leader is constantly in control, but everyone is allowed to contribute freely.

Leaders are most effective when they delegate well and fairly, when they ask questions more readily than they impose answers, and when they do very little of the speaking during the meeting itself.

3. *Follow-up*. Is your meeting successful? You can only define a meeting as a success when all of the elements are present. This does not mean only that it starts and ends on time, that your leadership skills were applied skillfully, or that assignments were given out. All of these attributes are essential, but they only lay the groundwork for the real action step. And that takes place after the meeting ends.

One of the leader's greatest responsibilities is to ensure that assignments are completed. You can delegate effectively, set deadlines, and believe that your meeting was a great success. But that is true only if the attendees come through. Thus, the leader must be able to monitor projects in the days and weeks following the meeting and make sure that others perform as promised. You probably know already that people don't always respond willingly. But as a leader, you must also be prepared to deal with differences of opinion about what assignments were given out in the meeting. Even when a specific request is made and an assignment is accepted, you might find that some people's perceptions change after the meeting. So as a leader, your follow-up task requires careful and complete communication not only during the meeting, but also well into the future.

LEADERSHIP TOOLS

Good leaders must be good planners and organizers, and persistent but diplomatic after-meeting monitors as well. Before, during, and after the meeting, you will need to take steps to build the features that will make your meeting succeed. Most important are the physical environment of the meeting, materials needed to make it work, and the agenda.

Physical Environment

Be sure your meeting will be held in an appropriate setting. Avoid a busy area, such as the floor of your department, where many people pass through, phones ring, and other disruptions draw attention away from the business at hand. Reserve time in your office if there is enough room, or in a conference room or other semiprivate setting.

Materials

Will you need to photocopy reports or prepare charts or graphs or other visual aids? Will you need a flip chart, blackboard, or other communication tools? Make sure that everything you and your attendees need will be on hand. If you are depending on others to supply materials, make sure they will be available at the meeting.

Example: A manager called a department meeting to review one employee's report. However, as the meeting started, the manager discovered that the report was not yet done.

Example: A manager was scheduled to make a presentation to the executive committee, concerning trends in one product line. She prepared a number of graphs showing product volume in various markets. These were sent out to be photocopied as pass-outs and also reduced to slides. As the hour of the meeting approached, the photocopies and slides were not on hand. She called the art department and asked about the status of her visuals, only to discover that her only copies had been lost.

Agenda

A specific and limited agenda adds validity and helps ensure that meetings are essential.

Example: A manager whose department was broken down into five sections called supervisors together to be briefed each week. From the manager's point of view, this was a necessary and positive session, because all supervisors came together in the same room. The manager believed this was the most valuable opportunity for communication and "working together" in the department.

The individual supervisors had a completely different point of view. In reality, because there was little interaction between sections, each of the five supervisors was wasting his time while the other four were speaking. As a result, they all resented this weekly meeting and would have preferred individual status meetings with the manager.

In this example the manager (the leader) had one purpose in mind, which was not being achieved. He had a different perspective on the meeting than did the supervisors. However, no one brought the problem out in the open—you cannot expect attendees to honestly criticize any meeting you call that they think is unnecessary or unproductive. People can't always be expected to risk telling you the truth, especially if you are their manager.

You might believe you're calling a meeting with the best of motives. You want clear, open communication; to give others the chance to speak out; to come up with solutions that everyone can agree with; or to demonstrate the fact that you're an enlightened manager. To test these assumptions, review your proposed agenda. First ask yourself, Can any of these issues be resolved away from the meeting, on a less formal basis? Then ask, Is the agenda complete?

In regard to the second question, a complete agenda—one that will best outline what everyone needs to know—should contain several elements (see Figure 2-1):

1. *Title.* Give the meeting a title. This helps clarify focus and the range of topics to be discussed. It also helps attendees identify and distinguish your meeting from other meetings they will attend, to help you expand or limit the agenda, to give you ideas for others who should be invited.

2. *Time and location.* Include the exact time, date, and place of the meeting. If you will be using a conference room, be sure you have reserved it before announcing your location and as part of your preliminary consultation. Include both the starting and ending time of the meeting, and plan to stay within those parameters.

3. *Theme and definition.* Write a brief description of the meeting's central theme. Define the problem or range of problems you plan to deal with in the meeting.

4. *Attendees.* List the names and departments of the people you have invited. Indicate which of the people listed is the meeting leader.

Figure 2-1. Elements of the agenda.

```
1. Title

2. Time and location

3. Theme and definition

4. Attendees

5. Topics:
        a. title
        b. description
        c. goal
```

5. *Topics*. Each agenda item should include three specifics: (a) a brief title for each agenda item, (b) description of the problem(s), and (c) the goal you want to accomplish during the meeting.

Example: You call a meeting to coordinate several departments' roles in completing a new monthly assignment. You are concerned with two major issues: the deadline problems this new assignment has created, and the specific responsibility for providing needed information. The figure on page 28 shows how the agenda for this meeting could read.

This format is more useful to attendees than the more traditional agenda, which simply lists topics by title or brief description. When your agenda lays out the program for attendees, you have a better chance of controlling the course of the meeting, keeping the discussion on the subject, and arriving at solutions.

AGENDA

Title:

New monthly assignment
—productivity analysis

Time and Location:

9:00 to 10:30, February 16
conference room, second floor

Theme and Definition:

Management has asked the accounting department to submit
a monthly report, which will require information from three
other departments. This meeting has been called to coordinate this task.

Attendees:

Martha Anderson, marketing
Bill Carson, accounting (leader)
Mark Leigh, sales
Barbara Ralston, administration

Topics:

1. Title: Deadline Problem

   Description: The deadline management has imposed creates a scheduling problem for several departments.

   Goal: To resolve deadline problems involved with the new
   assignment, satisfactory to all departments involved,
   and to ensure timely completion of the monthly report.

2. Title: Responsibility

   Description: Several departments are depended on to
   supply information needed for the report.

   Goal: To identify information each department will provide,
   and to agree on deadlines.

THE TONE OF YOUR MEETINGS

Preparation should be aimed at the attendees and their own objectives. As long as attendees benefit (by solving problems, identifying pitfalls, or clearing up a misunderstanding, for example), they will be more likely to work with you during future meetings. The tone of the meetings you call is set by the successes of past meetings.

Meetings are appropriate in these situations (see Figure 2-2):

1. *Problems are common to the group.* When you call a meeting of people who face a shared problem—one that requires working together to arrive at a solution—you should expect results. If the agenda affects only *some* of the people at the meeting, then either you have invited people who shouldn't be there, or you don't need a meeting at all.

Example: One manager applied a critical test to every meeting he called and every agenda he constructed: Everything on the agenda had to

Figure 2-2. Reasons to call a meeting.

1. **Problems are common to the group.**

2. **Information is needed in both directions.**

3. **Decisions are to be made collectively.**

4. **Responsibility is not clear.**

5. **The group wants to meet with you.**

be of essential interest to the people in attendance. Whatever did not pass the test probably didn't belong.

2. *Information is needed in both directions.* Information can and should flow in both directions. Either you want information from the people you invite, or they want and expect information from you. As long as the information does flow both ways, the meeting has a valid purpose.

Example: One leader had a dismal series of meetings, characterized by poor response from attendees. In thinking over the meetings, he looked for a common thread or fault and finally stumbled on it: He had been trying too hard to give attendees a great deal of information—but without making it work in both directions. As a result, he ended up doing all of the talking and not allowing anyone else the chance to take part.

3. *Decisions are to be made collectively.* Managers must make tough decisions, often on their own. But in some cases, you will want to involve subordinates or other managers in the decision you make. This is a courtesy when their working lives will be directly affected by the decision. But when it's something you should decide, and you prefer a consensus or approval, a meeting is not justified.

Example: A leader brought up an issue to employees in his department. "I know this is a decision I will have to make," he stated, "but my decision will affect all of you. I want to hear your opinions." His final decision was based to a large degree on the observations he gained from giving employees the chance to speak out.

4. *Responsibility is not clear.* You might have a task or project to complete that requires cooperation from several departments or individuals. You know from past experience that working with several information sources is difficult. Thus, a meeting's purpose might be to bring together each person who is involved and to clarify individual responsibilities.

Example: A marketing manager wants to promise a faster delivery date to customers. But to do so, he will have to ensure faster order processing, shipping, and other cooperative services from many departments. He makes this request during a management meeting, on the premise that the company will place itself in a better competitive position by speeding up its fulfillment process.

5. *The group wants to meet with you.* Some meetings take place not because of the leader's initiative, but because the group asks for it.

Example: The employees in a department ask the manager to call a weekly staff meeting. The manager complies and soon discovers that several problems remain unresolved within the department. The meeting serves as an opportunity to discuss them. As a result, several problems are resolved, and internal conflicts are lessened.

There are a number of circumstances in which a meeting is not justified, including the following (see Figure 2-3):

1. *Issues require singular communication.* Never call meetings to discuss issues that concern only one participant at a time. Meet with each person individually when practical. This takes up the same amount of your time, but doesn't waste the time of everyone else.

Example: A vice-president used to meet with all managers at the

Figure 2-3. When not to call a meeting.

1. Issues require singular communication.

2. You don't have a specific agenda.

3. Issues should be discussed privately.

4. Another form of communication is better.

5. A decision has already been made.

beginning of the week. This meeting took up the entire morning, a commitment the vice-president was willing to make. However, he soon realized that he could meet with each one individually and in the same amount of time, get more accomplished, and take up less of the attendees' time.

2. *You don't have a specific agenda.* You can surely depend on a poor meeting if you have not prepared yourself. You must have clear objectives, and you must invite only those people who need to be there.

Example: A manager felt compelled to meet with the entire department once per week, to discuss anything of importance. But when nothing presented itself, the meeting proved to be a waste of time. He abandoned the weekly format and called meetings only when specific issues needed to be discussed together.

3. *Issues should be discussed privately.* Some issues do not belong on the agenda for an open meeting. If you are having difficulty with an employee, a meeting is *not* the place for a confrontation. And if you need to resolve questions of salary levels, termination, or other sensitive and confidential material, save it for a more private setting.

Example: During a budget review meeting, a vice-president asked one manager why his department's payroll expenses were budgeted to fall in the third month of the new year. The manager was planning a layoff, but did not want to discuss it publicly. He responded, "This involves confidential information. If we get together after the meeting, I'll explain."

4. *Another form of communication is better.* Can you get the answer you need with a brief one-to-one session? Or with a letter, memo, or phone call? If so, take it off your agenda. Adopt the attitude that eliminating subjects from your meeting agenda is a sign of progress; adding more to the agenda will only lengthen the meeting and make it less efficient.

Example: A manager has an especially long agenda for a meeting that's supposed to take only two hours. In studying the agenda, he is able to eliminate four of seven items. They can be resolved with a separate, smaller meeting, with a memo, or with individual action.

5. *A decision has already been made.* Never ask a group for ideas or suggestions if you have already made your final decision. If members of

the group disagree with your conclusion, you'll only end up fighting them, and that's not productive. Besides, a group will see through this appearance of teamwork, which is a waste of time as well as a misrepresentation.

Example: One manager made the mistake of asking attendees to help resolve a problem. When the consensus of opinion was to take a course of action the manager didn't like, he argued for the alternative; finally, he admitted he had already decided. This harmed his reputation in the group.

ACTIVE AND PASSIVE LEADERSHIP

Adopting a low-key stance is not the same as being a passive leader. Low-key leadership means that you do not inhibit others from participating and that you don't have the attitude that it's *your* meeting. Passive leaders, in comparison, have no direction, no control, and in some instances, no agenda.

An active but low-key leader is always in control and achieves the best results by throwing ideas to the group and encouraging decisions. In order to achieve this, you must approach a meeting's objectives from several points of view (see Figure 2-4):

1. *The organization and its objectives.* Any decisions or actions proposed or finalized during a meeting—like all forms of corporate activity—must conform to the organization's overall purpose. If the meeting's course strays from this, it's doubtful that any decisions will stand. One problem you face as a leader is that not every organization has a clearly stated or well-undestood objective. Rather than proceeding on assumption alone, you must take the responsibility—as a meeting leader—to seek and then communicate the objective.

Example: During a meeting of managers in a nonprofit association, one person suggests entering into a program for the development of literature to be sold to members and to the public. The meeting leader compliments the idea, but suggests that the material should be distributed without charge—in consideration of the organization's objective.

Figure 2-4. Meeting perspectives.

1. **The organization and
   its objectives**

2. **Departmental goals**

3. **Individual priorities**

4. **The team interest**

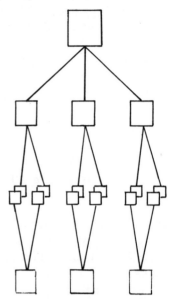

2. *Departmental goals.* What are the goals of departments that are represented in your meeting? If you invite managers from five or six different departments, they not only have an interest in agenda items presented in your meeting but they also have their own points of view, priorities, and interests. A successful leader is aware of differing goals and ensures that each point of view is heard, respected, and considered as part of the final decision for each issue.

Example: One agenda item during your meeting concerns the question of who should prepare departmental budgets. The consensus is that each manager should be allowed to present his or her own budget; but you are aware that the accounting department feels the need for centralized control. So you propose that each manager do the initial version, subject to overview and coordination by the accounting department.

3. *Individual priorities.* Every person in the meeting has an agenda of his or her own. This may be in conflict with the corporate objective and

with the departmental goal. However, this does not mean the individual priority is wrong or inappropriate; there are cases when the consideration of individuals is more important than the organization and its parts.

Example: Several attendees suggest that reporting procedures be altered in order to simplify them. You are aware that to do so will eliminate one person's job entirely. As leader, you raise this point and attempt to resolve the problem so that no one's position is adversely affected.

4. *The team interest.* The organization is, in a sense, a team. So is each department. A meeting, though, is a team of a special type that exists only during the session itself. Whenever a team is convened, a collective interest exists, as well as a series of conflicting departmental and individual interests. As leader, you must reconcile the differences and emphasize the similarities, in order to get results.

Example: You lead a meeting of several managers. The one agenda item concerns the problem of meeting an especially tough monthly deadline. Each department contributes information to the final report, but each perceives the task differently. Your role must be to focus the shared interest of getting the report done on time and of resolving the differences the individuals or departments have.

These meeting perspectives begin with a singular point of view (the organization), then expand to departments, and again to individuals. Then the team perspective narrows the point of view and task actions again become a singular idea (assuming everyone in the meeting can agree on the definition of the problem). This expanding and contracting scope defines how every meeting leader must focus the attention of the people in attendance.

THE PREMEETING

Besides speaking with attendees before the meeting regarding the agenda, plan to resolve as many problems as you can in advance. This idea works especially well when one other person will have to work with you, but the overall group will be affected by the final decision.

Example: You put together a meeting to coordinate the deadlines for a new assignment. One other department head will be especially interested in the outcome, since you will depend on that department to supply you with a good deal of the information you need. Before the meeting you get together with that department head and work out guidelines for the deadline. From this premeeting, you discover that:

- Some information can be prepared in advance.
- Certain reports now being prepared can be delayed so that this deadline will be met.
- Minor revisions in the new report could save many hours of work (for this idea you will have to get approval for modifying the report, a step that should take place before your meeting).

The premeeting also defuses any potential power struggles of the type that sometimes come up during formal meetings. Avoid surprises. You can expect others to react negatively when they're taken by surprise during a meeting. If you plan to make a suggestion that will have a direct impact on another department, see the manager well before the meeting. Discuss the idea. Ask for thoughts, alternatives, and reactions. You might not resolve the problem, but at least the other person will know your position.

If you expect worthwhile participation in your meeting, give attendees the information and time to prepare. Only then can you expect to reach your goals during the meeting. Never withhold information from someone else because you fear it will be controversial. Bring everything out in the open, and attendees will respect you for your professional approach. You can survive even the strongest disagreement with people who come to your meetings; but you do not need to accumulate enemies. You create antagonism by springing surprises, and you build alliances by demonstrating openness and trust.

WORK PROJECT

1. Name two good reasons to call a meeting, and explain why a meeting forum is required to resolve the issues that will be involved. Why is the meeting more effective than less formal communication?

2. Describe two cases in which a meeting is not required, and explain how a one-to-one meeting will be more effective in resolving the issues.

3. List the five sections of the complete agenda, and come up with a sample of what they should include.

3

The Invitation List

The length of a meeting rises with the square of the number of people present.

—Robert K. Mueller

The vice-president, while speaking to a manager who was organizing his first meeting, tactfully tried to make a point. But the manager didn't seem to get it. Finally, the vice-president explained, "When the Titanic was sinking, there weren't enough lifeboats for everyone. So what did they do with all the people left on the ship?"
"I don't know. What?" the manager replied.
"They called a meeting."

Determining who to invite to your meeting is one of the preplanning steps required of every meeting. Just as a social gathering works best when the invitation list is planned carefully, every meeting will be more successful if the right people are invited.

A chronic flaw in many recurring meetings is that the invitation list grows. A leader might believe that once someone has attended his weekly meeting that person must be invited every subsequent week. Otherwise, the person will feel insulted or threatened. This is simply not the case. Motivated, sincere managers or employees will appreciate being invited to the meetings where they can participate intelligently; but they will also become frustrated if expected to attend meetings of no interest to them or their department.

Example: One very well meaning president called several meetings per week. He was a creative, energetic leader who dominated meetings and inspired those who worked for him. Unfortunately, he also enjoyed being surrounded by his team, and the meetings became more frequent and better attended. This took key executives and managers away from their other duties, so that valuable time was spent listening to others talk. The accountant sat in on a marketing strategy meeting, the data processing head listened to a sales forecasting discussion, and the marketing director listened to a three-hour strategy session between the president and the corporate counsel.

WHO TO INVITE, AND WHY

Whether you call your meeting to solve a problem or a series of problems, check the status of work, inform the attendees, or get work done, always apply a test to determine whether or not the people you plan to invite need to be there. View the subject of the meeting in terms of components. What components (people) do you need to resolve the issues that will be raised during the meeting?

For problem-solving meetings, ask: *Who are the people I need to have on hand to arrive at solutions or who will have a direct interest in the solution?*

Apply this standard in selecting your attendees: Everyone who attends your meeting should benefit in some way. Even when you build the agenda, you must ensure that all of the people in the meeting (a) need to be there, (b) have a direct interest in the issues, and (c) are able to contribute information, ideas, or solutions essential to your purpose.

For status meetings, ask: *Who is directly involved in and responsible for scheduling and work execution? Who directly influences the progress of the job?*

This is an easy test to apply, and one that helps you remove unneeded people from your attendance list. It also avoids wasting other people's time by asking them to attend meetings in which they cannot participate, and in which they have no real interest or concern.

For information meetings, ask: *Who needs to be informed or, when I seek information, who has the information I need?*

Some meetings are called to announce new policies or new information when an interoffice memo would suffice. Avoid meetings for passing information that does not require response or interaction.

When your meeting is called to get information from others, ask yourself, *Who has what I want, and will I get the information during a meeting?* You might conclude that a one-to-one, less formal meeting will work better in many cases.

For work meetings, ask: *Who will work directly on the project and must be there?*

The most restricted attendance list should be the one for a work meeting. Some jobs must be performed in a group, and a meeting will be called as an actual work session. When you call such a meeting, clarify that it will not be a discussion period but a work period. Then be very careful in selecting the people to attend.

A work session cannot include anyone who will not contribute directly to the process you intend to follow. Chances are that a meeting of this type will be limited to two or three people. When your attendance level rises above three, it's unlikely that you'll get any results.

LIMITING THE LIST

As a meeting leader, you must employ tact whenever you exclude people from a meeting—especially when they expect to attend.

Example: The manager of personnel announces a meeting to discuss expected staff increases during the coming year. She invites three managers to attend. A fourth manager hears about the meeting and asks to be included.

At this point the easy response is to add the fourth manager to the attendance list. However, there is no good reason for him to be there. The personnel manager may respond with her reason for excluding him:

"There's no plan for expanding your staff this year. I invited only those managers who have asked for staff increases in their latest budgets."

The meeting leader may also ask others why they want to attend. What do they plan to contribute? What agenda items are of concern to them? Can their problems be addressed in a separate, smaller meeting?

Including or excluding people can be used as a way to make a political statement. Avoid this by being constantly aware of your reasons for (a) calling meetings in the first place and (b) deciding who should be there.

Example: The president of a marketing company called management meetings at least once per week, to discuss a range of subjects. Most department heads attended these meetings regularly. One manager, who was especially outspoken, criticized a program the president proposed during one meeting. His name was dropped from subsequent invitation lists.

THE SECONDARY MEETING

If someone wants to be included in your meeting, but has an interest in only a small portion of the agenda, you can solve the problem with one of several ideas:

1. *Hold a separate meeting.* Carefully select those who are needed for the agenda items the one individual wants to discuss. Hold a small, short meeting for that issue only. Make up this time by removing the issue from the agenda for your larger meeting.

2. *Invite partial attendance.* Move the topic to the top of the agenda, and invite the person to attend that portion of the meeting. With this idea, he or she can return to other work, without taking the time to sit through a lengthy agenda of topics that are not of concern.

3. *Recommend a separate meeting.* Another alternative is to suggest to the person that he or she should call and lead a separate meeting. This alternative allows the excluded person to devise a special agenda focused on issues he or she must deal with, but that don't interest the larger

group. This also enables the person to skip your meeting, thus saving time.

Participating in and recommending additional meetings can lead to excessive bureaucracy, and that's worth avoiding. Be aware of the time you spend in meetings, as well as the meeting demands you place on other people. Balance the meeting and work time so that excessive meetings can be avoided. Two ideas to achieve this are:

1. *Combine meetings.* If you are planning a series of related sessions with the same mix of people, can two or more of those meetings be combined? Avoid duplicating the same discussions in two or more meetings, and strive for economic use of meeting time.

2. *Eliminate discussion by means of premeetings.* You might be able to save time for the majority of attendees by taking care of one complex issue before your meeting. If you can meet with one other person to resolve an issue on a one-to-one basis, that will save time for all other attendees.

Meetings and related submeetings will take up a lot of your time. By applying the above ideas, you can make more efficient use of your day.

Example: A budget review meeting was called for all department managers. Its starting time was 10 A.M., and scheduled completion was noon. Because certain managers wanted preliminary and follow-up meetings, the leader's day followed this schedule:

   9—Premeeting with accounting manager
   10—Budget review meeting
   12—Luncheon meeting with personnel manager
   1—Follow-up meeting with marketing manager
   3—Follow-up meeting with accounting manager

Everyone has days like this. However, it's possible that some of the secondary meetings could have been combined, handled in a shorter time span, or eliminated. Many of the secondary meetings we attend concern political issues rather than work issues. And while that might be necessary due to circumstances in your corporate culture, such meetings often waste time.

When an attendee asks you for a separate meeting, ask these questions:

1. *What do you need to discuss?* If there's no good reason for a separate meeting, try to get out of it. Chances are that the person's agenda will fit within the context of the meeting you've already planned. He might request a separate meeting to be sure he gets your attention, to try to influence your opinion or position, or simply from force of habit. In many instances you will be able to resolve the problem with a brief chat at the time the separate meeting is requested. In essence, you have the meeting informally, and it takes very little time.

2. *Why can't we cover it in the regular meeting?* Secondary meetings waste time because they duplicate effort. Chances are that at the primary meeting you will have to go over the same material that you discuss beforehand.

3. *Who else should be in on the discussion?* When you're asked for a separate meeting, ask this question. You will find in many cases that the topic is appropriate for the entire group, because others will have positions to state. Suggest delaying the discussion until everyone is together. In this way you avoid duplicating the same material for two separate groups.

You can avoid the equally time-consuming follow-up meeting by concluding your agenda properly. Before you adjourn, ask, "Does anyone have any comments, questions, or points we haven't covered?"

When you get responses to this, be sure the issues relate to agenda items only. Otherwise, your meeting will deteriorate into a general discussion on anything and everything. You do not want this to occur, since it defeats your purpose in (a) limiting discussion, (b) sticking to the agenda, and (c) resolving specific problems.

If someone does raise a point off the subject, tactfully interrupt and suggest that it should be brought up later—in another meeting, on a one-to-one basis with the right people, or in some other forum. Remind attendees that the agenda—and everyone's time—is limited.

This technique does not always work. One manager asked the concluding question and received no response. But immediately after closing the meeting, three people approached him and asked for a private meeting. In all cases, their interest related to the overall agenda. This is unavoidable, for a couple of reasons:

1. *Fear of speaking out.* Some people have valid comments or suggestions to contribute, but they are intimidated during the meeting. In this case, gently encourage them to speak out *during* the meeting, to overcome their hesitation, and to contribute with a higher profile. At the same time, respond to the issue raised in a positive manner and with suggestions for follow-up action and solutions.

2. *Afterthought.* Some attendees will develop ideas many hours or days after a meeting has concluded. They should be heard, if only as a courtesy, but also because their contribution will be valuable. Some ideas are developed only after considerable thought.

EVALUATING THE LIST

How can you judge your own effectiveness in selecting attendees? Good leaders constantly question and evaluate their own performance, invite criticism from others, and revise their procedures.

Follow these criteria to judge how well you put together a meeting, and whether or not you invited the right people:

1. *Accomplishment of purpose.* Did your meeting achieve what you expected? If you're frustrated because the agenda couldn't be completed on time, no decisions were made, or you couldn't control the direction the meeting took, review your attendance list. You probably had the wrong people—and too many people—at the table.

2. *Comments from others.* Did attendees complain about the meeting? Did it take too long, were the discussions inapplicable, or did you fail to exercise the leadership the group required?

When no one approaches you, ask a trusted peer or friend to critique your meeting for you. Listen to what he or she tells you, and identify ways to improve your preparation and performance next time.

3. *Frequency of meetings.* Do you need to call meetings on a frequent basis? Can you reduce the number of meetings you lead? If you suspect that you're involved in too many meetings, chances are you're right. Look for ways to combine gatherings, eliminate some of the attendance, and shorten the time that each meeting requires.

SUGGESTING CUTBACKS

The corporate manager who recommends cutting the number of meetings—or reducing any other form of bureaucracy—takes a chance. Many people will resist your attempts to simplify procedures. It's human nature to resist change, even positive change. So suggesting a *reduction* in meeting activity requires sensitivity and great care.

Remember your motive: to save time and effort, reduce the number of people going to meetings, and cut the frequency of meetings held. As long as you constantly refer to your purpose, any criticism of your idea can be better addressed in the context of what's good for both the company and each person who attends meetings.

Example: You have suggested eliminating a weekly project status meeting. Your reason: The long-term projects discussed during this meeting are monitored in another monthly meeting, and this is duplication of effort. However, the immediate response from some other managers is that the weekly meeting is essential. You make your point by modifying your original idea: A weekly meeting should be held *only* if a project runs into trouble and immediate action is required to correct a problem. Otherwise, the monthly review should suffice. This compromise is acceptable to everyone.

It might be impossible to eliminate all of the meetings you perceive as unnecessary. However, even if you combine two meetings into one or do away with a single meeting each week, you will improve the situation. And whenever someone suggests creating a new meeting, either on a one-time basis or permanently, always question whether it's necessary.

In too many cases, calling a meeting is an excuse to avoid action, when the solutions you seek do not demand a gathering of many people.

INVITATION LIST ACTION PLAN

Keep these important steps in mind when you are planning your invitation list:

1. *Be aware of perceptions concerning meeting attendance.* If you do exclude people, speak to them directly, and explain your actions.

2. *Remain flexible.* It might be a wise move to invite people who want to attend your meeting, even if you don't think they need to be there.

3. *Reduce the time required for your meeting by holding smaller, one-to-one meetings whenever possible.*

4. *When topics come up that do not concern your entire group, suggest that others hold premeetings and then report to the group in summarized form.*

5. *Don't allow recurring meetings to grow in attendance size. The most effective, efficient meeting will decline in value as the invitation list expands.*

6. *If some individuals ask for a separate meeting, ask them what they want to discuss that could not be handled with the entire group. The resulting dialogue often will take care of the issue.*

7. *Recognize the need for separate meetings in some cases.* Certain attendees might fear speaking out in front of others, have an afterthought of value to you, or need to discuss something in confidence.

WORK PROJECT

1. What questions should you ask when compiling a list of attendees for

a. problem-solving meetings?
b. status meetings?
c. information meetings?
d. work meetings?

2. List the questions you should ask when attendees request a separate meeting with you, and explain how your question helps eliminate the secondary meeting.

4

Staying in Control

Frank complained, "I have a lot of trouble running my meetings, but I'm not sure how to solve the problem."

His friend Mark answered, "The solution isn't that tough. You just have to let them know who's in charge. Be a little more assertive."

Frank thought it over for a moment, then asked, "But what if they won't let me?"

Everyone who leads a meeting must face the problem of control. This does not mean that you should control the people in your meeting. The degree of "control" you exert does not refer to your style, nor to the perception others hold of you as a meeting leader. We define control as how effectively you are able to keep discussions on agenda topics, delegate responsibilities to attendees, identify and give out assignments, and follow up to ensure that promised work is completed. Regardless of corporate rank, a meeting leader must assume responsibility for these goals. They might require asserting your position, repeating or clarifying a point, or striving for careful and complete definition.

Example: A heated debate during one meeting was going nowhere. Each side had a specific point of view and would not compromise. The leader gently interjected a question about the exact nature of the problem being hashed out. The response opened up the dialogue and revealed that each side was talking about a completely different problem. Once the leader brought the discussion around to the point at hand, the two sides found that they were in complete agreement.

SETTING GROUND RULES

You have the right and the responsibility to set reasonable ground rules for your meeting—not a series of strict rules that *must* be obeyed, but standards aimed at allowing the participants to achieve common goals. An overly strict environment inhibits discussion and expression and will only create dissent in a meeting.

Example: A leader suggested guidelines and announced them. These related to length of the meeting and the topics that would be discussed. In addition, during the meeting, he attempted to keep discussions on the topics at hand and constantly tried to lead attendees toward final decisions and solutions to problems.

There are two levels on which control must be achieved: first, on the assumed level that you will lead the meeting, even when attendees outrank you; and second, in dealing with attendees in general and enforcing the commonsense rules for good meeting conduct.

Leading while superiors are present might prove to be a challenging experience. When you are given the assignment of presiding over a meeting at which your boss or another executive will be present, a few ground rules will certainly help to defuse what might otherwise become an uncomfortable and ill-defined situation.

Example: One manager was inhibited during the meeting because her supervisor attended. She feared that if she was overly assertive her supervisor might stop her. But then she discovered that by concentrating on the agenda and not the personalities, she was able to lead the meeting and achieve its goals.

In attempting to set standards for your meetings, your purpose must be to create an orderly environment, one in which a positive and successful interaction will be allowed to take place. Any gathering of people requires a degree of order. It might be limited to an overall agreement that the leader or chairperson will recognize someone who wants to speak (this is a more formal rule of order, more appropriate for committees than for business meetings).

The business meetings you lead will probably be less formal than a committee gathering, where motions are forwarded and seconded and a specific number of rules always apply. It's more likely that you and your attendees will sit around, take turns speaking, and allow one another to finish a thought without interruption. In such a setting, your leadership role does not extend to control over who speaks or what is said. Instead, your purpose is to resolve agenda items, including appropriate assignments and follow-up; monitor projects and tasks that come out of the meeting; and plan for future meetings with the same group.

These goals are best achieved in a less formal setting, where the leader provides the role of controller. You need to ensure that the agenda is addressed, that discussions do not wander too far from the stated topics, and that participation among attendees is balanced.

Ground rules for meetings should include the following (see Figure 4-1):

1. *A preannounced agenda.* Always prepare your agenda before the day of the meeting, and make certain that everyone who will attend has a copy for review.

Others may argue that meetings cannot be so well organized that you know a day in advance what will be discussed. Your best argument against this is, "A meeting must be organized well in advance, or we're not ready to meet. Everyone who is invited to attend must be given time to prepare. That's the only way to create a productive meeting, and the best way to ensure worthwhile results."

Example: One manager was not able to get an agenda finalized until just before the meeting time. As a result, attendees were not completely prepared to discuss every topic. The following month the manager made a special effort to get the agenda completed and distributed to all attendees a few days before the meeting. As a result, the participation level was greater and the meeting took less time. The leader

Figure 4-1. Meeting rules.

> **1. A pre–announced agenda**
>
> **2. Verified attendance**
>
> **3. Uninterrupted meetings**
>
> **4. Adherence to the agenda**
>
> **5. Achievement of a specific result**
>
> **6. Identification of the meeting leader**

believed that the meeting's quality was vastly improved because of the prepublished agenda.

2. *Verified attendance.* You should know before your meeting begins whether or not invited people will be at the meeting. If your agenda subjects involve participation by people critical to your decision, they must be there—or there's no purpose to including that topic on your agenda.

Example: The leader was depending on one key person for two out of three items on the agenda. When that person did not show up, the discussion could not lead to a final conclusion. Thus, the majority of the meeting's goals could not be reached.

3. *Uninterrupted meetings.* When attendees are called out of a meeting to speak with someone or to take a phone call, that disrupts everyone else and often stops the progress you have a right to expect.

Your standards must include a provision for no interruptions. Actually, this should be a general guideline for all meetings in your company. That includes people coming in and going out while the meeting is in progress, phone calls tapped into the conference room, nonattendees coming in to ask questions or deliver messages, and any other form of disruption. You can achieve a good deal of cooperation with two steps: Hold meetings where no phone lines are tied in, and keep the conference room door closed during your meeting.

Example: A leader had been frustrated in the past because meetings were constantly interrupted. Even when employees were hesitant to enter the room, they called on the internal phone system, directly to the conference room. The leader began closing the door while the meeting was in session, and she disconnected the phone extension in the room. These steps reduced the number of interruptions during subsequent meetings.

4. *Adherence to the agenda.* Your meeting should be designed to cover the topics on the agenda, completely. Avoid letting other topics come up, especially when that prevents you from completing your agenda items. There are exceptions, of course. In the discussion of one topic, an urgent related problem might arise and you will have to let the discussion take its own course. But look for times when the discussion wanders too far from your intended course, and then gently bring the meeting back to the agenda.

Example: One leader was especially effective in making sure all agenda items were covered in the time allowed for meetings. But occasionally a discussion led to a topic not on the agenda. If this was important enough to deviate from the plan, the leader did not try to interrupt. To avoid missing important agenda items, he was sure to put the most critical topics at the top of the agenda, leaving less important subjects to the end.

5. *Achievement of a specific result.* You must communicate the purpose of your meeting and plan to achieve that purpose. Most meetings are flawed in this regard—the agenda is described as "to discuss the budget" or "to discuss (a specific) problem." But discussion, while a process during the meeting, is not the purpose. A specific result is to *solve* a problem or make a decision that can lead to action.

Set goals and communicate them to your attendees. Specify the positive *results* you want to achieve through your meeting—decisions, actions, and assignments that are necessary for solving problems.

Example: A leader saw a great improvement in her meetings when she started writing agendas with specific goals. Rather than describing an agenda as "to discuss budget variances," she listed it as "to identify causes of budget variances and devise procedures for closer expense monitoring and control." This led more easily to solutions.

6. *Identification of the meeting leader.* It's very difficult for attendees to participate when the leader is not clearly identified. Be sure that attendees know who is leading the meeting. Achieve this with two steps. First, see everyone you invite to your meeting before the meeting actually takes place (to involve them in the agenda plan). And second, identify yourself on the agenda itself as the leader. You will also establish your position by being the one who leads attendees through the agenda, listens well, asks questions, suggests follow-up actions, and gives assignments as the result of discussions.

Example: One leader had become uncomfortable during last month's staff meeting, because it seemed that no one was sure who was running the session. In putting together the agenda for the following month, the leader was identified by name. In addition, he met with each attendee in advance and discussed how each person would participate in the meeting. During the meeting, he concentrated on the agenda itself and attempted to keep discussions flowing toward solutions.

While you might agree that these rules make sense, there is still the problem of communicating them. For example, you are given the assignment of calling and leading a meeting. Attendees will include several other managers, as well as executives who outrank you. How do you communicate your meeting guidelines to all of your attendees, and how can you ensure that those guidelines are followed?

You can best demonstrate meeting leadership by creating and planning a well-focused agenda, by communicating directly with attendees in advance of the meeting, and by always keeping your goals in mind. You are meeting to address specific issues, to identify solutions, and to assign responsibility for follow-up actions. A leader who takes this approach will gain respect from attendees, as well as enthusiastic participation.

Leaders who want to run meetings in a positive, productive environment will be able to meet their goals when they apply the guidelines for orderly meetings. And that should be your intention as a leader.

CREATING PARTICIPATION

A leader must be able to create a forum in which people feel free to participate. This will require a good deal of planning, thought, and positive encouragement of attendees.

Both vocal and nonvocal attendees can make a valuable contribution to your meeting. However, as the leader, you are in a position to balance the participation factors. The vocal group must be allowed to speak, as long as they do so within reason. And the more passive group must be asked to comment, to present ideas, and to take assignments.

Example: You are running a meeting with six attendees. Two are doing most of the talking and have specific points of view and ideas on each topic. The other four sit passively and offer no advice. As each topic is introduced, you explain the problem and ask for ideas. The same two people speak, and you allow them to do so—ensuring that their comments are on the topic. But then you also ask the others to comment or state their own ideas.

This balance must be achieved within the time frame you have allowed for your meeting. If you have a total of two hours and there are four major areas to cover, you must be aware of how long a discussion is running. You must also be able to stop the talk and arrive at a solution soon enough so that the remaining agenda has a chance, too. If you begin running over your time, it might be necessary to introduce a topic and immediately ask for comment from one of the more passive members of the group—instead of allowing the more vocal ones to take over and dominate.

Another way to create participation is to speak before your meeting with a few of the passive attendees. Take an agenda item of particular interest to them and let them know you plan to turn a segment of the meeting over to one of them. Let a passive person make a report, present ideas, or make a proposal for a change in procedures. Then others in the meeting—including yourself—can ask questions, disagree, or offer alternatives.

If you are forced to do most of the talking during your meeting, you are not allowing or encouraging others to participate well enough. A meeting is least effective when a group of attendees sit passively while you present ideas and do all of the talking. When this occurs, ask yourself these questions:

1. *How can I encourage others to participate more in the meeting?* Your job as leader is not to run the meeting in strict accordance with a set of rules, but to create a forum in which action and effectiveness are made possible. Your real task as leader is to get others to contribute something of value.

Example: A leader was aware that one attendee rarely spoke out during a meeting. But in one-to-one sessions the individual expressed thoughts clearly and had many excellent ideas. To encourage greater participation, the leader began asking for that person's opinion during the meeting.

2. *What topics are of special interest to specific members of the group, and how can I get them to present their ideas?* A good leader makes sure that everyone having something to say gets a chance, that the right people make the right decisions, and that participation is shared by the attendees on a fair basis. The effective leader has the appearance of doing little more than keeping the meeting moving from one topic to another.

Example: The meeting leader was dissatisfied with the results of a recent meeting. In thinking back to the format and level of participation, she realized that she had been too vocal herself. In a subsequent meeting she tried speaking less and asking questions more. The emphasis was on reaching final decisions, rather than on stating opinions and ideas.

3. *Do I enforce the rules so strictly that no one is willing to speak up?* If you live by the rules so completely that others are unwilling to speak out, you defeat your purpose. You must be able to achieve the results you want with as little effort as possible. This means that any time you stop someone from speaking you use great diplomacy and sensitivity and that people feel free to speak out at your meetings without the fear that you'll interrupt them or prevent them from speaking.

Example: The leader was angry because many of the attendees showed up late for his meeting. Resisting the temptation to say anything, he went through the agenda and extended the ending deadline beyond the planned one, cutting into the lunch hour. When one attendee complained about this overrun later, the leader explained that the meeting didn't start on time, because several people showed up late.

CONTROL ACTION PLAN

Follow these steps to create the best meeting environment for your attendees:

1. *Establish guidelines and not rules.* Concentrate on encouraging adherence to those guidelines rather than on an enforcement posture.

2. *Stay in touch with your attendees.* See them before your meeting and plan their participation in advance.

3. *Always refer to the agenda to change the direction your meeting is taking.* Avoid personality issues and emphasize the importance of reaching the well-stated goals of the meeting.

4. *Indicate start and stop times for your meeting and make every effort to operate within those restrictions.* But remain flexible, recognizing that not every meeting can conform to those restrictions.

5. *Allow discussions to proceed away from your agenda when a secondary topic is urgent.* Recognize that some discussions will lead to other issues that must be resolved. Even with a well-planned agenda, the leader cannot always know in advance what will be covered in each and every meeting.

6. *Verify attendance.* If some attendees are essential to a particular agenda item, ensure that they will attend and that they have planned their own level of participation.

7. *Encourage everyone at your meeting to add something of value.* Create participation by meeting with people in advance and structuring a segment of your agenda for their interests. Let an introverted person take over that part of the meeting, present a report, or make suggestions.

8. *Tactfully control participation during your meeting.* If one or two people are doing most of the talking, ask others for their comments and ideas. Strive for a balance.

9. *Review your leadership role critically.* If your meeting is not achieving its purpose or if people in attendance do not speak up, ask yourself

whether your leadership posture is overly aggressive, or if there are steps you can take to improve your own performance.

WORK PROJECT

1. Explain two rules for leading meetings, and tell how these rules help you to lead effectively.

2. How should you propose rules for meetings, and what can you do if management does not approve of your ideas?

3. What questions should you ask yourself when there is no participation during your meeting?

5

Following Up: Unfinished Business

A committee is a thing which takes a week to do what one good man can do in an hour.

—Elbert Hubbard

"We have a problem here," Peter said. "At last week's meeting, several people agreed to complete assignments, but none of them came through."
"What happened?" Ted asked.
"I spoke with a couple of them. They said there wasn't enough time to do what they promised, because they've been busy attending other meetings."

A leader must lead not only during the meeting, but afterward as well. The steps you take in following up ultimately will determine whether your meetings hold lasting value for the company. Merely giving out an assignment is not enough; the leader must also take the initiative to ensure that the assigned person or department comes through as promised.

By taking the right steps during and after the meeting, you will be able to ensure timely completion of assignments, even when someone who outranks you is given the job. While you might be responsible for identifying what must be done, you must be able to prod others into actually following through on their promises.

GETTING RESULTS FROM MEETINGS

No matter how much discussion takes place, and no matter how completely the attendees at your meeting agree on the steps that must follow, a meeting is *not* successful or productive until action is taken. In fact, the meeting exercise is not complete until the follow-up action has occurred. A lot of would-be productive meetings end up as conceptual exercises. Why? Because nothing comes from the effort.

Set a standard for yourself. As a meeting leader, you must see to it that everyone accepting an assignment completes work by an agreed-on deadline. This is achieved with several steps (see Figure 5-1):

1. *Lay the groundwork well before the meeting*. When you first begin to identify the people who should attend your meeting, speak to them in terms of assignments they are likely to receive. This must happen before the meeting itself.

Example: A manager is organizing a meeting for the following week. She visits the marketing manager and says, "We'll be discussing the problem with the income forecast. As you know, we're well below the original estimate, and a revision is needed. Will you be prepared to take that assignment?"

With this preliminary step, the attendee will not be taken by surprise. He will begin thinking in terms of the revision—or at least he has the opportunity to object.

2. *Make specific assignments*. One reason actions often don't result from a meeting is that assignments are vague. The responsible person might depend on help from others, and they might not come through.

Every assignment must be made as directly and specifically as possible, the degree of responsibility must be verbally clarified and

Figure 5-1. Guidelines: getting results from others.

1. Lay the groundwork well before the meeting.

2. Make specific assignments.

3. Write it down and send it out.

4. Send copies to the right executives.

5. Follow up in person.

6. Ask for help.

7. Use the most dependable resources.

agreed on, and any secondary involvements must be cleared up at the meeting.

Example: During a meeting one manager agrees that a job should be completed in his department. A week after the meeting, the leader visits with the manager and asks how the project is going. The manager is surprised and responds, "I didn't realize I'd accepted an assignment. I only agreed that, *if* the assignment was made, it belonged in my department."

3. *Write it down and send it out.* Summarize all assignments given and accepted, in the form of a memo. Send the memo to everyone who attended the meeting, and ask for responses. Those people who have agreed to deadlines should be expected to respond specifically.

Attach a note to the general memo, asking for confirmation of these points:

- The exact nature of the assignment
- Secondary involvement
- Deadline

Ask the responsible person to let you know at once if there will be a problem in coming through as promised.

Example: The leader concluded his meeting, having given out several assignments. However, one attendee seemed vague in his responses, so the leader followed up with a confirming memo. As it turned out, the attendee was *not* certain about the assignment or its deadline. The memo helped clarify what had been agreed on.

4. *Send copies to the right executives.* Don't overlook the chain of command. As a meeting leader, you are responsible for letting your supervisor know what's going on. And in some cases, you must also contact supervisors of those who accept assignments from you.

This comes up when someone agrees to do a task for you, but subject to the approval of a supervisor. You can help explain the nature of the project by submitting an explanatory memo to the executive or manager involved, summarizing what was discussed at the meeting and asking permission to make the assignment.

Also summarize each meeting you hold with a memo to your own supervisor. Let your boss know what you're doing, what decisions were made, and what reports or tasks you expect to be completed by others.

Example: After a decision-making meeting, you write to the vice-president who oversees the work of several managers in attendance. You summarize the tentative assignments made and ask for permission to proceed. In the event there is an objection, this courtesy prevents bad feelings from developing later.

5. *Follow up in person.* You must expect to have some problems getting responses to memos. Some people simply don't read them, or else they conclude that no action or response is required.

With this in mind, plan to follow up all internal correspondence with a personal visit or telephone call. Ask the other people if they've had a chance to study your memo, whether they have any proposed changes or clarifications, and if they agree with your conclusions and plan of action.

Example: The leader had made a number of assignments during a weekly meeting, including some to other managers who reported to separate divisions. To clarify what was agreed to, he sent a confirming memo to each person who was given an assignment. A few days later, he also called each one to confirm that the summary expressed in the memo was correct.

6. *Ask for help.* Every meeting leader will eventually face the difficult problem of discovering that someone else is not going to come through on a promised assignment. In this case, the best approach is to meet with the unresponsive attendee and ask for his or her help.

Explain your problem and need to have the assignment completed by the agreed-on deadline. If he will not be able to comply with your request, ask if he needs help from someone else. Offer to help in any way you can and, in return, ask for his help, too. Failing that, you will have to conclude that the task is not going to be done. Avoid giving critical assignments to the same person in the future.

Example: After your meeting, you contact a fellow manager who accepted an assignment. You are told, "I won't be able to get that done by your deadline." You ask whether she needs extra help or more time. But it becomes evident that she's simply not going to do the job. From this you conclude that you cannot count on her help in the future.

7. *Use the most dependable resources.* Even with all of the steps above, there will be instances where nothing comes from your meeting. Some people will simply not come through, even after making a promise. Unfortunately, some attendees do not take meetings seriously. To them, nothing that's agreed to in a meeting really counts.

Learn from this experience. Depend only on those people you know will come through on their promises. And when putting together the attendance list for future meetings, remember who can be depended on and who cannot. This will dictate the list of people worth inviting.

Example: One leader built a core of dependable fellow managers who always came through on promises. When an especially difficult task with a short deadline came up, he knew who could be counted on to come through, and he made the assignments accordingly.

In addition to following these steps, don't make your plans a secret. Let everyone know exactly how you intend to proceed in ensuring that assignments come through—as promised and on time. As long as you act in good faith, you will not alienate anyone or make enemies. You will simply become a more effective and successful meeting leader.

THE NEED FOR IMMEDIATE START-UP ACTION

A meeting leader cannot afford to let time slip by. The need for immediate action cannot be overstated. This applies not only to deadlines, but also to setting starting times of assignments.

When you give someone an assignment, and when it's defined and clarified, you must ask, "When can you get started?" If the other person wants to delay for a week or more, ask for reasons. State that you'd prefer an immediate response. As a general rule, keep in mind the tendency to let things go with time. *The longer the gap between the assignment and the beginning of a response, the less chance it will be done at all.*

When you get someone to commit to starting on a job the same day, or the next morning, you can also ask for an earlier deadline. Regardless of when the individual promises to begin work on an assignment, the deadline must be stated clearly.

KEEPING MINUTES

Your task is to ensure successful and timely completion of work—the action that must come as the direct result of holding a meeting. This goal may be destroyed by poor communication, not only among attendees but from you as well. The solution to this problem is to keep minutes of your meetings.

Example: During discussions in your meeting, an assignment is given and agreed to. The deadline comes and no results are turned in. When you visit the manager who agreed to complete the work, you find that his recollection of what went on during the meeting is completely different from your own.

Keeping minutes will not completely undo this problem. You must also state assignments as clearly as possible, and ensure that the person on the receiving end has just as clear an idea of what's expected. The minutes, along with your follow-up memos, support this communication; but a record of your meeting can only be as specific as the communication that occurs. The value of minutes is that they can be sent to each attendee as confirmation of what was concluded. Ask someone to attend your meetings with the sole purpose of recording everything that occurs. The minutes should not be a transcript; they must only be concerned with the following points (see Figure 5-2):

- *Date and time.* When did the meeting take place (date, starting time, and ending time)?
- *Attendees.* Who was at the meeting (name and title of each person, identification of leader)?
- *Agenda topics discussed.* Describe the topic briefly.
- *Definition of problems.* Include one or two sentences stating the issue.
- *Alternatives presented.* What ideas were offered and who offered them? Include brief comments or major points, and the name of the person stating them.
- *Solutions agreed on.* What was the outcome? Explain the actual solution the meeting attendees agreed should be acted on to solve the problem.
- *Assignments made and accepted.* What people were given the assignment? If they attended, state that they acknowledged and accepted the task and that they understood the assignment; if they did not attend, comment that a follow-up contact is required.
- *Deadlines.* When will the work be done? Does this include a contingent deadline?
- *Follow-up actions.* What actions must be taken after the meeting? Who is responsible? Who will monitor follow-up, and how will it be reported to the responsible person?

The person who takes minutes must be aware of what you want included. Write up a sample set of minutes and go over your guidelines with your meeting secretary.

Figure 5-2. Outline of minutes.

```
—date and time

—attendees

—agenda topics discussed

—definition of problems

—alternatives presented

—solutions agreed on

—assignments made and
 accepted

—deadlines

—follow—up actions
```

By having one person working only on the minutes who is not involved in the meeting discussion itself, you will be able to ensure a complete record of your meeting. The purpose of minutes is to ensure clarification and understanding, to provide a running record of decisions and how they were reached, and to remind people before subsequent meetings what projects are under way.

The minutes should be typed up as soon as the meeting has concluded, and sent to every attendee. Also send the minutes to selected executives when appropriate, including your supervisor and the supervisor of each person who accepted a tentative assignment. Be sure to let everyone at your meeting know who will get a copy of the minutes, so that no one will be taken by surprise.

The minutes should be simple and straightforward in their design. Anyone who reviews the minutes should be able to tell, very quickly, what went on during your meeting and what follow-up actions are expected to occur. The figure on page 67 provides an excerpt from some minutes, showing how they should be constructed. The minutes improve communication for you and for everyone who attends your meetings. This document prevents the misunderstandings that often arise within hours or days after a meeting; and it prevents someone from interpreting what was discussed and what conclusions—if any—were reached, in any way that differs with what was clearly stated and agreed on during the meeting.

REVIEWING AT THE NEXT MEETING

An assignment given one month should be reviewed in a subsequent meeting. This step is an important one. Even if a job has not been completed, it gives you and your meeting group the chance to review progress.

The problem of poor follow-up can be observed time and again in recurring staff meetings. The leader asks attendees to take care of a problem, look into something, or report back—within the week or month, or as soon as possible. The attendees do not comply, for whatever reason.

The problem is compounded when the leader fails to follow up at the next meeting. If you run a monthly staff meeting, for example, your first agenda item should always be a review of assignments given during the previous month. Send your agenda around early to those who will attend. When they see that the first order of business will be to get an update on *their* assignment, that could be the single fact that gets them to act.

DELEGATING ASSIGNMENTS

The leader must organize, define, and create action. And the leader must also be an effective delegator of work. If you find that you end up doing

Topic: Procedural change, monthly status reporting

Definition: The meeting leader explained that monthly status reporting does not provide a means for clear identification of problems.

Alternatives: The leader proposed a revised format for reporting, with emphasis only on projects running behind schedule and procedures for taking action.
    The marketing director stated that status reporting should be performed by each manager and that the current centralized procedure is inefficient.

Solutions: The consensus of attendees was that reforms are needed in methods of reporting project status.

Assignment: The accounting manager accepted an assignment to write a report proposing reforms, since his department currently prepares the companywide report.

Deadlines: The report is due two weeks from the date of the meeting and will be copied and sent to all attendees for discussion at the next meeting.

Follow-up: The meeting leader promised to speak with the accounting manager after the meeting, to help develop guidelines for the report.
    The accounting manager stated he will contact each manager during the next three days, to obtain ideas for revised procedures.

most of the follow-up on your own, then your meetings are not working. Apply these rules for effective delegation (see Figure 5-3):

1. *Identify responsibility*. For each agenda item ask yourself, "Who is reponsible for this assignment?" If it's you, then it probably doesn't belong on your agenda in the first place. Thus, as a general guideline, you should be able to delegate every assignment to someone else.

Example: One leader dreaded meetings because he ended up with more work each time he met with others. Finally, he was so overloaded that he stopped to consider his leadership style. He realized that he was failing to delegate. From that point forward, he set the standard for himself that, with few exceptions, all work coming out of an agenda would be delegated to someone else.

2. *Don't turn delegation around*. Never let someone else delegate assigned work back to you. In many meetings the initial assignment fails

Figure 5-3. Rules for delegation.

1. Identify responsibility.

2. Don't turn delegation around.

3. Ask attendees who should do the job.

4. Don't overload any one person.

5. Beware of the silent attendee.

6. Acknowledge a job well done.

and the leader ends up taking it back. This means you're overloaded, and others learn that if they don't come through you'll do it yourself.

It's a sign of good leadership when you identify the person who should do the job. And by the same argument, it's a sign of ineffective leadership when you end up doing everything on your own. No one holds any sympathy for the martyr—and you don't do yourself any favors by becoming one.

Example: One leader made assignments and tried to follow up with each person. But when someone else did not come through by a promised deadline, the leader readily finished the task himself. Once others realized this would happen, they stopped trying to complete assignments at all. Finally, the leader realized what the problem was, and he took a more assertive follow-up stance.

3. *Ask attendees who should do the job.* Don't delegate without consulting the group or, if you already know who to appoint, say as much and then ask for other opinions. When you get someone else to accept responsibility, your job of ensuring follow-up action is made much easier—because the job was accepted rather than imposed.

Example: The meeting leader had a poor experience with delegation and concluded that it wasn't as easy as others seemed to think. The problem, though, was that he imposed assignments on others, often at random and without consultation with the group. Once he stopped doing that, the delegation phase became easier.

4. *Don't overload any one person.* Watch out for those attendees who are too eager to accept assignments. If someone volunteers for extra work, that's a positive attribute. But if a person wants to do everything and anything, he will end up with so much to do that he won't do any of it well.

Example: One attendee volunteered for a large number of assignments. The leader limited the amount of work that employee was allowed to accept and directed several assignments to other attendees.

5. *Beware of the silent attendee.* On the assumption that everyone in attendance has a valid reason for being in your meeting, it's also fair to assume that each person will do his or her share. Look for the individual who never accepts an assignment, and ask yourself why. Should this person be included in your meeting at all?

Example: You have led a weekly meeting for the last three months. Two of your attendees never volunteer for projects you have to give out, although they are quite vocal in criticizing policies and procedures. You change this by assigning work to them on issues they complain about—on the assumption that vocalizing is the same as volunteering. The result: The previously silent members end up doing their share of the work and speaking up more selectively. Criticism, you conclude, is fine—as long as the critic is willing to take constructive action to solve the problem.

6. *Acknowledge a job well done.* When someone comes through with the completed assignment, on time and in the format you wanted, let everyone know how much you appreciate his work.

Example: At the beginning of a monthly staff meeting, the leader always starts out with positive comments. He names those people who completed assignments from the previous month and thanks them. Everyone wants to be appreciated. Announcing successful actions shows your awareness and makes you the best type of leader—one that others want to please.

UPWARD DELEGATION

Even if you agree with the ideas for delegating assignments to others, you might be uncomfortable with the thought of asserting that process with an executive. When an attendee in your meeting outranks you, delegation takes on an entirely different look.

Upward delegation requires a different approach than one you can use with a subordinate. When you make an assignment to a subordinate, you can simply say, "Get this done by Tuesday. If you have any problems along the way, see me at once." But you cannot give the same message to a vice-president.

You can achieve the same result, though, when dealing with someone who outranks you. Upward delegation is easier than most people think, for one reason: *As long as you delegate with tact, even a high-ranking executive will respond well.* Here are some examples of how this can be achieved:

Example: You want to ask a vice-president to complete a report and present it at the next meeting. He is the obvious choice. You ask, "Who should do this report, and when should it be completed?" The executive responds that he will do the job, and that it will be ready by the next meeting.

Example: You have an assignment for a divisional chief, but hesitate to give it directly because he outranks you. So instead you say, "I think this task should be completed in your division. If you'll give me the name of the person I should contact, I'll be glad to give him the details he'll need." The divisional chief reponds, "I'll take care of it myself."

Example: You decide to take the direct approach. You ask a vice-president, "Shouldn't you take care of this job? I know you've done similar studies in the past." The vice-president agrees and promises to come through during the following month.

A first step to take before attempting upward delegation is to identify obvious responsibilities. Then, when you do ask an executive to accept the assignment, you're less likely to meet with resistance.

Example: While discussing a problem, the vice-president comments that procedures must be changed. As a preliminary step, he says, the proposed changes should be summarized in a report. At this point, you—as the leader of the meeting—must ask, "Who should do that report?"

The stronger the executive's opinions, the more likely he will answer, "I'm the one." As long as someone else believes he is best suited to see the job through, you'll have little trouble getting him to accept your assignments.

The real problem is not in delegating upward, but in following through. For example, what actions can you take when an executive accepts an assignment and then misses the deadline?

Example: The executive vice-president attends one of your meetings, proposes the solution to a problem, and then promises to take action. However, in checking with his office a week later, you are told that other priorities have made the deadline impossible to meet. The same excuse is offered twice more over the next month.

The solution: There's not much you can do to force an executive to act. It's inadvisable to go above his or her head (for example, sending a memo to the president to complain that a vice-president did not come through). You can take other steps, though:

1. *Ask for a meeting with the executive.* Explain your problem, but also be prepared to offer an alternative. This should include reassigning the job, so that it does get done. With this idea you are offering to remove one task from the busy person's schedule.

2. *Insist on a decision.* There's nothing more harmful to the successful progress of an assignment than indecision. If you run into someone who won't let go of an assignment, but who also fails to complete it, confront the problem. Ask for permission to give the job to someone else, or propose ways to get it done as soon as possible.

3. *Remember the experience.* The next time that executive sits in on one of your meetings, avoid delegating critical assignments in that direction. If the executive does volunteer, construct the job in such a way that other managers are involved in the assignment. Look for ways to minimize the executive's time commitment by shifting responsibility to other attendees. This not only avoids a repeat of past problems, but it also helps minimize the workload for someone who outranks you.

Your task as meeting leader should not be to burden yourself with a lot of extra work. The best way to tell whether you're doing the job well is to measure your meetings in terms of how well work has been delegated. The fewer obligations you end up with as a result of your meetings, the more effectively you lead.

Your real task is one of monitoring. You invite the right people, define problems, get solutions narrowed down to specific assignments and deadlines, and then keep your eye on progress. You ensure that the lines of communication remain open and that others come through with promised assignments. That's where the successful leader really gets to work.

FOLLOW-UP ACTION PLAN

Take these steps to ensure effective follow-up after your meetings:

1. Remain constantly aware, before and during your meeting, of the need for follow-up. Include as part of your meeting plan a schedule for follow-up actions you will take.

2. Make assignments as specifically as possible, including the exact deadline.

3. Whenever you give someone else an assignment, send a confirming memo as soon as possible after your meeting; then call or visit in person to again confirm the assignment and the deadline.

4. Whenever you give an assignment to someone outside of your reporting chain, be sure to confirm the assignment—both with the individual and with that individual's immediate supervisor.

5. Be aware of who is a dependable resource. Use people you can depend on to complete critical assignments.

6. Avoid giving assignments to people who do not come through. Or, if you think a second chance is in order, be careful in selecting the work you do assign.

7. Always follow up immediately. Remember that the greater the gap between the meeting and your contact, the lower the chances work will be done—especially if there is a breakdown in communication and understanding.

8. Keep minutes of your meetings, to highlight the decisions made. Minutes serve as a reminder to everyone in attendance of what was decided. They also help ensure continuing communication.

9. Learn how to delegate well. Never impose a job on someone else, but ask the right questions. That makes delegation easier and more successful.

10. When you delegate to someone higher in rank, phrase your request carefully—in the form of a question or gentle suggestion rather than an outright order.

WORK PROJECT

1. What are two guidelines for getting results from attendees at your meeting? How do these guidelines make your meeting more productive?

2. Describe information that should be included in the minutes of every meeting you hold. Explain how this information is beneficial in follow-up.

3. List two rules for effective delegation, and tell how they make the leader's job easier.

6

Politics for Leaders

If you want to make enemies, try to change something.

—Woodrow Wilson

Pat telephoned a fellow manager and started out, "I didn't ask you to attend next Monday's meeting, but only because there was no good reason for you to be there. I'm sure you understand."

He paused and then continued. "You're taking this very well. A lot of people would have been very upset at being left out . . . hello?"

When you assume the role of leader, you must not only make sure that the meeting is structured for action, that the agenda is complete, and that you stay in control. You also need to be aware of how others will react to everything you say and do, and even to the message you send out by *not* asking someone to attend.

During the meeting itself, you need to be aware of how others react to your comments, questions, and answers. Every action and statement you make is observed by your attendees; and to a greater degree, what goes unsaid will send out a message to the people you invite and to those you do not invite.

The political environment that rules your corporate culture dictates how people perceive you as a meeting leader. In some situations you will be able to undo negatives by honest communication; in other cases you must take great care to avoid placing yourself in a politically volatile situation to begin with.

One way to keep the political climate healthy is to make sure everyone speaks up and contributes. Make your meetings democratic by encouraging participation.

PARTICIPATION: THE THEORY

Leaders create participation through their meetings, and you have the chance to define and then act on this opportunity. But you must first decide what teamwork really means, what its purpose is, and what results you expect from it.

Participation should work, given a series of assumptions we make about other people. But those assumptions are not always applicable, so getting a team to work requires leadership and hard work. The assumptions include these ideas:

- People are more comfortable on a team than when they are expected to act independently.
- A group of people benefits from sharing ideas.
- A team achieves more than an individual will be able to.

None of these beliefs are always true; more often than not, they are false. One study, conducted by psychologists at the University of Tübingen in West Germany, concluded that because only one person can speak at a time, people contribute fewer ideas in groups than they arrive at on their own. And in a study of juries, researchers at the Center for Advanced Studies in the Behavioral Sciences in Palo Alto, California, found that larger groups take longer to arrive at decisions and that those decisions are identical to those reached by smaller groups.★

Participation is a worthwhile idea, or there would never be a need

★"Recent Studies Help Explain Why Some Meetings Fail," *New York Times,* June 7, 1988.

for meetings. And achieving the benefits of participation is worth the effort required of every leader. These benefits include:

1. *Involvement.* Even when meetings are less efficient than independent or limited action, there is a considerable intangible benefit to be gained from them. When many people are involved in the decision-making process, morale and self-esteem are maintained and improved—assuming that people are truly allowed to contribute and are not merely tolerated as they take part in the *appearance* of participation.

Example: A leader asked attendees whether the weekly meeting should be discontinued. All attendees responded that the meeting was too valuable to disband. After the meeting had ended, one of the group approached the leader and told him, "I've been in a lot of meetings, but this weekly session is responsible for bringing me out of my shell. Don't stop holding this meeting."

2. *Communication.* A lot of effort in meetings is expended in taking the time to arrive at a decision and then in communicating that decision to people who were not in the meeting and correcting the misconceptions that arise as a result. A meeting is efficient when everyone affected by a discussion and solution attends and takes part in the outcome. Otherwise, the time you spend planning and running a meeting will only be the beginning; you will have to spend much more time correcting the damage created by poor communication outside of the conference room.

Example: One manager did not attend a weekly meeting, but was expected to produce a report that resulted from discussions. The leader had much difficulty summing up the discussions for the manager after the meeting had concluded; the manager would have been wiser to attend.

PARTICIPATION IN PRACTICE

Meetings can easily end up as the symptom of a poorly structured internal organization. Then "participation" no longer means working as a team toward common goals, and progress cannot take place. The team becomes a forum for avoiding responsibility or blame, rather than a group of individuals who share interests and want to solve problems.

Example: A group meets to discuss a problem in completing assigned monthly work on time. Instead of identifying the actual source of the problem, comments point to flaws in other departments, and the discussion does not do anything to resolve the issue. Without this required definition, the meeting adjourns with only one resolution: that all departments must "work together." In fact, this is a nonconclusion that will not lead to any positive results.

If you want your meetings to be the exception to the rule, and if you want participation to work for you, be prepared to function from very specific guidelines. Use the group to collect ideas, hear alternatives and dissenting opinions, and offer to provide needed help in completing a project. But always insist that, in the end, someone will be responsible for completion of a specific, well-defined task—not the group or even two people, but one primary individual who must account for the success of a project, or for actions that will solve a problem.

Follow these guidelines:

1. *When discussions get away from the desired result of coming up with solutions, remind the group of their purpose—to define the problem and come up with a solution.*

2. *Identify the person with primary responsibility to act.* Your job as leader will be to support that effort and to ensure that the goal is reached.

3. *Make a distinction between blame and responsibility.* As long as discussions are exercises in placing a blame, your meeting cannot progress. Look for signs of this occurring, and then tactfully direct the discussion toward solutions and constructive action.

4. *When an attendee claims that someone who is not at your meeting must take charge of a solution, proceed with caution.* Don't settle for that reasoning. It only means that the meeting cannot achieve its goals. As long as you have carefully selected your attendees, the group should be able to identify the causes of problems and, thus, arrive at a solution.

Participation Through Quality Circles

As a meeting leader, you can organize your participative group with some of the guidelines used by quality circles, but perhaps with a less formal degree of organization.

The quality circle is an idea originated in Japan in the early 1960s by Dr. Kaoru Ishikawa, an engineering professor at Tokyo University. Groups of employees meet periodically to identify, study, and solve specific problems common to their work area.

Quality circle participation is voluntary. This is one key element that must be in force during every meeting you hold. You can expect sincere participation only from people who want to be on the team. The quality circle is independent from the corporate chain of command, so that the appointed leader is in charge of organizing and running the meeting, even when members outrank that leader. The circle group agrees on specific objectives, decides to deal with defined problems, and sets deadlines for itself. It then assigns segments of the analysis or reporting task to individual members.

Participation groups like quality circles have been used effectively in more than 8,000 United States business and government organizations. Estimates are that approximately 90 percent of the Fortune 500 companies have quality circles or groups like them in place.★

Circles were widely popular during the late 1970s and early 1980s, although it now appears that much of the growth of circle involvement was to some degree a fad. The experience curve appears to be initial enthusiasm and endorsement, followed by a period of constructive work, and ending with a declining level of interest. But in many organizations the quality circle has become a permanent factor in the institution, with many positive results for employees and for management.

Those companies that invest in training circle participants are likely to realize profits. A survey conducted by the Quality Circle Institute concluded that for every dollar spent to pay employees while attending circle meetings, two to three dollars were saved through cost-cutting ideas or suggestions to increase profits, offered by circle committees.†

★"Quality Circles After the Fad," *Harvard Business Review,* Jan./Feb. 1985.
†"Largest Quality Circle Survey Ever Conducted Produces Surprise Findings," Quality Circle Institute news release, Sept. 1984.

The savings come from ideas and suggestions developed and rec-
ommended by quality circles. This is one example of a well-structured
team being created to solve problems, and producing positive results.
Management has traditionally responded poorly, or even with apathy,
to the notes dropped in suggestion boxes—often because suggestion
boxes are frequently used as ways to allow employees to vent their ideas,
when management hasn't the slightest intention of responding. But
when an organized team of people recommends changes to management,
backed up with research and proof, those changes have a greater chance
of being listened to and implemented.

Managers in companies where quality circles and other participative
programs have worked well not only support the program wholeheart-
edly; they also respect the opinions of their rank and file. Managers
believe that the employee is in the best position to understand his or her
work environment and to make suggestions to improve procedures and
conditions. Elitist managers, in comparison, have no respect for employees nor for their ideas and will never be able to create a constructive
environment for participation on any level.

The recent history of quality circles as applied in business gives a
good indication of how every meeting leader can create a truly effective
team. You do not have to institute a formal quality circle program, with
all of the training, cost, and structure that involves. But you can benefit
from employing the same guidelines that have made quality circles work
in many situations.

Most important among these guidelines are

1. *Common interest.* Every member of the team must share the same
concerns, face similar problems, and be in need of solutions. The most
obvious expression of this idea is to restrict each circle to participants in
the same department or section. This is the same point that you face in
inviting the right people to your meeting and excluding those who
should not be there. In your role as a leader, though, you must solve the
problem of excluding people in a different way—because some meetings
lack the precise definition of the quality circle program.

Example: You are frustrated because past meetings have not been
able to solve problems on the agenda. But on review, you see the
problem: The people in attendance hold conflicting goals and points of
view. Not everyone in attendance has had a direct interest in the problems

under discussion. The solution: Structure future meetings with attendees who share common problems and are interested in developing solutions.

2. *Voluntary basis.* Participation can never be forced. It must be entered into because people want to work together. Quality circles are organized on a strictly voluntary basis. Your meetings would be much easier to run if this rule was always practical; but that is not realistic in many situations.

Example: You have had problems creating real and meaningful participation in your meetings. Some of the attendees have been ordered to attend, and they are not really interested in working on the team. You understand the problem and continue to encourage others to take part. But you also accept the unfortunate fact that not everyone will share your enthusiasm for the projects you want to assign.

3. *Specific, defined projects.* Just as quality circles concentrate on well-defined problems, every meeting you hold must have a clear purpose and must have a solution as the ultimate goal. The quality circle chooses its own tasks, by consensus. You cannot run your meetings in the same way, so you have to organize participants within defined limits. However, you can allow a degree of free choice in your meetings.

Example: You decide to apply the principle of free choice as far as you can. You are not free to select which problems to solve, nor to allow participants that much latitude. As an alternative, you invite ideas for solutions or approaches that might not be obvious.

4. *Clear leadership.* In the quality circle program, a leader is appointed regardless of rank. And during the meeting, that leadership is clearly established and agreed on. If you attempt to impose that degree of definition for your own meetings in a corporation, you will run into problems. Even though leadership should be clearly established and agreed on, the corporate culture recognizes formal title rank more than temporary meeting status.

Example: Your meetings are fairly informal, with attendees free to speak out on any topic on the table. You have recognized that it's impossible to impose leadership. Instead, you focus your attention on the agenda. This makes you the best possible type of meeting leader.

These guidelines make meetings work. In most business situations, similar rules for conducting meetings are rarely stated as clearly or even agreed on implicitly. Companies that succeed in taking action and using the meeting to define follow-up steps and solutions are characterized by well-defined, tightly structured meeting situations. And the attributes that are required for success—notably a clear agenda and a consensus of leadership—are essential to the equation.

SOLUTIONS TO THE TEAM PROBLEM

The politics at work in a company may restrict your actions to some extent; but that political climate also offers the solutions that you need in order to function as an effective leader.

The same factors than can lead to negative political attitudes and actions can be used to create the most positive meetings possible. In a highly positive political environment, communication improves with time. Having direct, honest communication with others is a powerful political weapon, as well as simply a good business tactic.

When individuals are functioning in a negative way, they avoid communication, plan and defend against real or perceived power threats, and spend a lot of time talking—usually to everyone except the source of their problems. You will take people off guard when you enter their department and engage in a direct and honest dialogue with them. By identifying the problems you face and probably share with them, it will be possible to arrive at mutual solutions.

A team can function only when interests are shared. In the negative political environment, no one wants to take the chance of sharing ideas with someone else, for fear of becoming vulnerable to "attack," or in the belief that someone will steal ideas and take credit for them. These are tangible concerns in a cutthroat situation, and the wise manager will be aware of the problem. But you can create a more positive and trusting environment.

Example: You ask an attendee to present an idea during an upcoming meeting. The attendee states he'd rather not, for fear that someone there will take the idea and claim it as his own. You allow that to pass without comment. But in the next meeting, you present a list of your own ideas to the group at large and ask for ideas, suggestions, and comments. By doing this, you demonstrate to the defensive attendee that you do not fear having your ideas taken by others. In fact, you encourage it, as long as the results are good for the organization.

The issue of authorship should not be tolerated in a positive team environment. While a good leader will single out individuals to acknowledge accomplishments, the insistence on owning an idea is contrary to the best interests of the team.

To resolve the conflict between the desire for power and influence among individuals, and the benefits of working as a well-motivated team, you must set an important standard for everyone who attends your meetings: All ideas belong to the team. If a particular individual is best suited to take action, that individual's success will be acknowledged.

Example: An attendee accepts an assignment and prepares a summary report for presentation at the next month's meeting. You are pleased with the response, so you send a brief memo to the attendee's supervisor, describing the experience in the most positive terms.

A team cannot exist merely because someone declares it to be so or calls a meeting together, appoints people to a committee, or even assigns responsibility. A team exists only through action, definition, and emphasis on the positive attributes of teamwork. It must be much more than lip service; you must demonstrate your leadership, and you must acknowledge contributions made by your team's members.

POLITICAL ACTION STEPS

Observe these guidelines for dealing with the politics at work in your corporate culture:

1. Never forget that people want to be included in decisions, discussions, and solutions. Keep this in mind at all times, but especially when thinking about excluding someone from your meeting.

2. Constantly review the attendance list for recurring meetings. Don't let attendance grow with time, if you want to maintain a smoothly running meeting environment.

3. Be willing to share information. People want to be informed, and their morale will suffer if they believe that information is being withheld.

4. Never discourage dissenting opinions. Only through dissent can you identify the conflict involved in a decision. By airing all views before making a decision, you will improve the outcome.

5. Emphasize decisions, action, and deadlines. As long as these are your priorities, your leadership during meetings will improve, and you will achieve the results you want.

6. Encourage real participation, based on the theories that have made quality circles worthwhile. Combine the best attributes of those programs with the less formal environment in your company.

7. Always recognize a job well done. Praise and a brief memo to an attendee's supervisor go much further than any other form of thanks.

WORK PROJECT

1. Compare the attributes of formal quality circles with the attributes required for less formal business meetings, in four areas:
   a. common interest
   b. voluntary basis
   c. specific, defined projects
   d. clear leadership

7

Time:
Managed or Wasted

It is a standing joke that when you become too senior to work, then your work is going to meetings.

—Woodrow H. Sears, Jr.

The meeting ran over its scheduled time, and one manager quietly excused himself. As he rose, he apologized to the group, "I'm already late for another meeting . . . on the subject of time management."

Everyone knows that business meetings can act as time killers, and if you don't control your attendance, you will become less productive, less effective, and less able to do your job.

The last few chapters were concerned with meetings from the leader's point of view. This chapter deals with the issue of time management and meetings, for both leaders and attendees.

Every meeting should be evaluated, both before and after, by one critical test: Is it necessary? That can best be defined in terms of problems and solutions. You must be able to identify the necessity of a meeting by asking whether or not it produces results.

In this chapter we will discuss the importance of time management for everyone who attends meetings, as a leader or as one of several attendees. You will discover that by applying the necessity test, you can quickly identify which meetings are worth attending and which only waste time.

THE ACTION APPROACH

You might discover yourself in a meeting dilemma. If one meeting leads to another, if you spend more time in a conference room than in your department, and if meetings seem to go well beyond their deadlines, chances are you need to be more selective in setting your schedule.

Example: A manager attended a running all-day meeting, starting at 8 A.M. and ending at 7:30 P.M. During the day he was given several assignments. The next morning the vice-president called a meeting at the beginning of the day and started out by asking the manager for one of the reports assigned the day before.

Obviously, if you're in meetings all day, you can't be expected to complete assignments you are given. In the example above, a look back showed how pointless it was to attend the all-day meeting. The manager did not have to be there, and his assignments could have been completed back in the department. The only tangible accomplishment of that day was the delegation for action; thus, attendance itself was largely a waste of time, unless it was necessary in order to develop the assignment.

If, at the beginning of the all-day meeting, the leader and the attendees had been able to agree on the premise for the meeting, several things might have been accomplished:

1. The meeting could have been shortened.
2. Several of those in attendance could have been excused.
3. Assignments could have been given early in the day and completed.

Unfortunately, many of the people who call meetings also have the hardest time formulating action, or even assuming an active role. And in many cases, you are forced into the role of attendee, whether you want to go to a meeting or not. It is not always your choice.

How can you deal with this problem? You do not want to confront an individual ordering you to attend or even lead a useless meeting, but you can confront and question the purpose of the meeting. Ask, "Why is this meeting necessary? What are we trying to accomplish here?"

As you find yourself sitting in a meeting and listening to others speak, ask yourself: Does this discussion affect me, in the sense that I can participate in the solution to a problem? In other words, is my participation necessary in order to define the problem, arrive at a solution, and give it a deadline? If not, then your time is being wasted. The focus of the meeting is wandering away from the agenda or from the stated premise for gathering people together.

Meetings tend to be oriented toward discussion rather than action. Your reaction to nonproductive discussion can be either to participate in the discussion (meaning you will help talk about a problem), or to challenge it (meaning you will demand decisions and action in a tactful and appropriate manner).

Something very interesting occurs when people stop discussing problems and decide to solve them. It's fairly easy to comment on problems in general terms. But demanding action is much more productive. For example, during a meeting, the discussion wanders away from the original agenda item. You speak up: "Who is responsible for solving this problem, and when do we want it solved?" One point of caution, however: If the meeting leader is not really interested in results, you may create resistance or antagonism by demanding action.

Example: A consultant was given responsibility for streamlining departmental tasks in a marketing company. He called a series of meetings for every department manager, which averaged four to five hours each and took place three times per week or more. One manager realized that the meetings were unproductive, since the consultant was merely discussing problems and not developing any solutions. He made the mistake of trying to force an action approach. Later, he realized that the consultant was not motivated to quickly cure the problem or even to define it. The manager realized that the consultant was being paid not for the project, but by the hour.

How can you deal with this problem? Depending on how much

clout the meeting leader holds in the organization, it could be dangerous even to raise the issue. Some ideas:

1. Look for opportunities to take positive action without making an enemy. Volunteer to put the leader's ideas into action. Chances are that a leader who is unable to formulate an action plan will respond well to this.
2. Submit a written proposal to the meeting leader, suggesting action steps in line with the ideas he or she has expressed during meetings.
3. Ask for deadlines. You may volunteer to work on a project, achieve an end result, and submit a report or devise a solution by a reasonable date in the future.

Example: A manager attends a series of meetings called by the vice-president, but no action is defined and no specific assignments are given out. However, several problems are raised and discussed. The manager prepares a memo and submits it to the vice-president. It outlines a series of projects aimed at solving the problems raised and offering to participate in those solutions.

You will never be able to please someone who is not motivated to achieve results. However, in the majority of cases, meetings are led by people who do want to solve problems and simply don't know how to go about it. If you can assume the role of a problem solver, and take an active part in formulating a solution, most of the people you meet with will appreciate your good efforts.

Theories of action, identification, and response do not always work easily. We must carefully construct the messages we convey in order not to offend others. The meeting may have a stated agenda. But be aware that the meeting leader and the other participants may have a point of view vastly different from yours. This may relate both to what the real issues are, as well as to opinions about how they should be addressed and resolved, either by individuals or by the group.

OVERCOMING MEETING FLAWS

Some meetings are too broad and general to address specific issues. For example, a weekly manager's meeting might be designed to encourage airing of problems, or as a chance to plan ahead and coordinate upcoming work projects. These meetings should be extremely short. In some organizations they may take an entire morning. In the interest of managing time well, make these points to your supervisor:

1. When several managers attend one meeting, the cost is high. Thus, the greater the attendance by supervisors, the shorter the meeting should be.
2. A time limit would help improve the use of time during meetings.
3. When a topic is discussed at length, little gets done in terms of resolution. As a solution, each agenda item should be introduced, explained, and then delegated to the appropriate manager for action—after the meeting has concluded.

The problem of meeting control versus participation requires planning and firm leadership. As an attendee, you might observe a meeting leader who is unable to find a working balance. And as a leader yourself, this problem is one that requires a lot of attention. However, it is critical to find the right balance, or a lot of time will be wasted.

DEFINING TIME PRIORITIES

The meeting's duration can be predetermined by exercising effective leadership and controlling the agenda. Some people might react negatively if an agenda is so overly detailed that the time for discussion of each item is listed separately. However, you can decide in advance how much time to allot to each topic.

As a leader, you should never hesitate to stop a discussion and go forward. You can achieve this with these techniques (see Figure 7-1):

1. *Keep the focus narrow.* Avoid general discussion and strive for focused solutions. As a leader, keep the issue at the front of your mind, and make sure attendees stay on the topic.

As an attendee, avoid taking part in lengthy discussions, and ask for definition and a course of action.

Figure 7-1. Time control techniques.

1. Keep the focus narrow.

2. Use the argument of time.

3. Keep follow—up notes.

4. Don't add to the agenda.

5. Stop on time.

2. *Use the argument of time.* As soon as the discussion moves away from the focus you want, put a stop to it by pointing out that the meeting is on a time limit. Say, "In the interest of time, we'll have to go on to the next topic." However, be sure the discussion ends with specific decisions concerning follow-up action.

3. *Keep follow-up notes.* Use meeting minutes to keep track of assignments and other follow-up action. A future meeting or, in some cases, supervisory follow-up, should be based on the decisions, actions, and deadlines determined and agreed on at the meeting.

4. *Don't add to the agenda.* Even with a complete agenda, every leader is eventually faced with the problem of unexpected business. If a crisis comes up, it might have to be added to the agenda. But most unplanned topics are not really emergencies.

Attendees can help keep a meeting on schedule by also paying attention to agenda items and by not bringing up topics other than those scheduled.

5. *Stop on time.* Even when the entire agenda is not covered, due to too much time being spent on earlier agenda items, try to stop the meeting on time. Put less urgent business at the end of the agenda, and try to stay within the time frame.

CONSTRUCTING THE AGENDA

The agenda serves more than one purpose. When properly used, the agenda helps in terms of the following (see Figure 7–2):

1. *Organization.* The agenda is an organizational tool. It helps you to plan and also helps your participants to prepare for the meeting. However, it cannot be limited to this role. The agenda provides much more.

2. *Preparation.* The agenda, when used properly, helps participants prepare for the meeting. With an agenda in hand well in advance, participants are in a position to contribute.

3. *Time management.* As a leader, you can use the agenda to plan the time required for a meeting, to identify the participants, and then to control the total amount of time spent on each topic.

Figure 7-2. The value of an agenda.

4. *Continuity*. Many types of business meetings are revolving exercises in project monitoring, or at least are intended to serve that purpose. Thus, during one meeting, an assignment is given to someone; and at the next meeting, that manager reports on the status of the job. The agenda for these meetings must include a discussion of new projects, but also must include a listing of status checks for work in progress.

LIMITING MEETING FREQUENCY

You might have observed that the more meetings you attend, the less gets done. This can apply not only to your own department, but to everyone who attends. Having a lot of meetings is rarely a sign of productivity.

The real work of an organization does not take place in meetings. The action center is the department, and meetings best serve action by helping to study and define its course. If a manager spends so much time in meetings that the department is not being led properly, then the amount and quality of work must suffer as a result.

Constantly look for methods to reduce the time spent in meetings, in three ways:

1. Eliminating meetings altogether and replacing them with less formal modes of communication
2. Holding certain meetings less frequently
3. Dealing with some problems between department managers, so that an attendance list does not have to include everyone

Avoid making these mistakes:

1. *Feeling obligated*. Don't attend a meeting only as a courtesy to another manager. There certainly are meetings you must attend, but in some cases you will have a choice.

2. *Adding to the problem*. If you find yourself in an unproductive meeting, don't add to its length by speaking out. This is one instance

where it's better to remain passive and not add to the problem—unless you see an opportunity to improve the meeting's tone.

3. *Failing to ask for definition*. Ask the purpose of a meeting before you go. We have emphasized meetings that are structured to solve problems, on the premise that every meeting should address issues and conclude with a solution. In practice, a meeting could be designed to train, to inform, or merely to brainstorm. As a meeting leader, be sure you understand the type of meeting you're calling, and define the goal you want to achieve.

You can make every meeting you attend a worthwhile and productive experience. But if you accept the wasted meeting as an unavoidable, unchangeable fact of life, then the problem will never be solved. Take an active role, not only in the way you participate in meetings and respond to the problem-solving process, but also in the planning and structure of meetings in general.

Besides managing time well and insisting that others respect your time, you will gain more benefit from attending meetings when you're well prepared. Remember that good preparation means you can fully participate in devising solutions to the problems a meeting will involve. Preparation is the topic of the next chapter, from the attendee's point of view.

WORK PROJECT

1. Name three techniques for controlling time, and give examples in a meeting environment.

2. Explain two benefits you receive by using an agenda, and describe how these benefits improve meetings.

8

Attendees: Before You Show Up

One manager arrived at the meeting room with a huge volume of material in hand. But when the vice-president asked him to pass out copies of one specific report, he could not find it. "I thought you said you were organized for this meeting," he whispered to the manager. "No," the manager answered, "I said I was prepared. I never claimed to be well organized."

If you want to have an edge during a business meeting, you must first know why it is being held; and then you must prepare *and* organize yourself before you attend. Take every meeting seriously enough to plan for, and don't make the mistake of merely attending.

As an attendee, you will be a valuable part of every meeting as long as you go with the intention of adding a productive edge. You can contribute a great deal to the purpose of the meeting by bringing something of value along: an informed opinion, important information, or a constructive idea. With these benefits, you may expect to participate in the best possible way.

PREPARATION TIPS

There is a difference between organization and preparation, but we tend to confuse the two attributes. Meeting attendees are organized when they understand the agenda and have formulated their own points of view. They may also be *politically* organized by knowing in advance where everyone else at the meeting stands on an issue, and often, by knowing when to speak out and when to remain silent.

Attendees who are prepared have taken the time to gather information before the meeting. This is not limited to making copies of reports, nor to reviewing the agenda and making notes about points to raise. The truly prepared attendee is one who both formulates a position and is ready to explain and, if need be, to defend it.

Example: An upcoming meeting includes an agenda item to cut 30 percent of your department's selling expense budget. You believe that this will directly affect future gross revenues as well as net profits. Your purpose in attending the meeting is to prove that the cuts are not justified.

Example: The vice-president of your division has called a manager's meeting to discuss an upcoming national convention. You plan to propose not attending, because you believe the cost of the convention is not worth the limited marketing benefits it provides.

In both examples, you can expect to meet with conflict and some very strong opinions on the other side. If you merely go to the meeting and argue your points, you will probably lose. However, if you take the time to prepare in advance, and if your points are valid, then you have a better chance of making your point.

Preparation will make your attendance productive and will improve the degree of influence you hold in the company. One of the greatest causes for frustration with meetings is that very few attendees make any

attempt to prepare by building proof for the points they want to make—
if they speak up at all.

The process of meeting would be greatly clarified if everyone would
prepare in advance; however, you cannot expect this to occur. By and
large, people who go to meetings do not make the connection between
professional work methods and the meeting itself. The most well-
organized manager might show up at a meeting without any preparation
whatsoever. This only frustrates your best intentions and the goals of
the meeting leader. Your fellow attendees may be willing to debate and
offer opinions, but few do their homework in advance of the meeting.

To prepare for your attendance, follow these steps (see Figure 8-1):

1. *Get a copy of the agenda.* As soon as you are invited to attend a
meeting, your first step should be to find out what will be discussed. If
no agenda has been prepared, find out all that you can. As we have stated
before, you must know what will be covered before you attend, or else
you are preprogrammed not to participate.

Example: You have been invited to attend a meeting early next
week. Your first step in preparation is to ask for a copy of the agenda. It
isn't available, so you ask the leader to give you a preliminary list of
topics. From this you plan to develop opinions and a position.

2. *Decide what is applicable.* Review each item on the agenda in terms
of the work you perform. How does the subject apply to you, if at all?
Will your department be affected by a policy decision? If the majority of
items on the agenda do not affect you, then you must question why you
were invited and how you can add value to the meeting.

Example: You are working on your budget, and that takes up most
of your time. When a fellow manager asks you to spend a morning in a
meeting, you ask for an advance copy of the agenda. None of the topics
seem to apply to your department. You call the meeting leader and raise
this point, only to discover that several points will affect your budget.
Now you understand why you have been invited.

3. *Formulate a position.* You hold a perception about what is best for
you, for the company, and for your department. Each agenda item in
which you hold an interest will affect these perceptions in some way. So
if you are to prepare in a constructive manner, you must be able to
communicate your position.

Figure 8-1. Preparation steps.

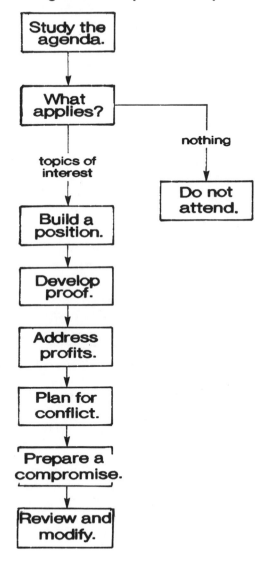

Example: In preparation for an upcoming meeting, you make several notes concerning each agenda item. These notes are organized in terms of how outcome will affect the work in your department, budgets, and use of personnel.

4. *Develop proof.* We must assume that an agenda issue is controversial and that various attendees will hold different points of view. Otherwise, why hold a meeting? If that assumption holds, then you must be prepared to argue your case, and that will require proof. If you take the time to document your point of view, then you will probably be far ahead of most other attendees.

Example: During a meeting you are prepared to argue your point of view. You have prepared a list of historical information for one agenda item; for another, you have investigated the outcome of a similar change the year before. With these facts in hand, you're able to argue your point of view strongly.

5. *Address the question of profits.* The best way to win your case is to present proof no one can dispute. In every business issue the question of profit is always present. The way that a decision affects the bottom line is invariably the guiding force for decisions. So always build your case around this issue. Point out the profitability connected with your point of view.

Example: The vice-president has proposed eliminating one product line on the basis that it is not profitable. However, you have compared the most recent income statement to a pro forma outcome if the product line were not included. You have discovered that overall profits would have been lower, because the product absorbs a portion of fixed overhead. With this information in hand, you are prepared to make a strong case for not eliminating the product line.

6. *Plan for conflict.* It might not be enough to prepare a strong case supporting your position. If you are familiar with the issues, then you already know the opposing viewpoint. Don't simply build a case for your side; also address the arguments you know the other side will raise. In fact, the strongest argument you can make is one that bases its best points on arguments of the opposite point of view.

Example: You plan to propose a change in procedures that involve several departments. You know the objections held by other managers, so you base your argument around those objections. By raising and explaining them and then showing how your solution reduces the problems involved, your own point of view is better presented.

7. *Develop a back-up position.* You will not always get your way. This does not mean you have failed, only that other considerations were stronger or that others in the meeting presented their point of view more convincingly. Prepare for this by developing a proposed compromise. If your point of view is not accepted, be ready to offer it.

Example: One item on this morning's agenda concerns contracting for a new, expensive automated system. You want to argue against getting this system, because you believe the company cannot justify the cost. In the event your position is rejected, you are prepared to suggest investing in a much less expensive hardware configuration that can be expanded later.

8. *Review and modify.* Review your success in meetings. How often do you win your point, and how often do you lose? What arguments did you not anticipate, and how can you do better at the next meeting? By constantly modifying the strategies and arguments you use, your meeting performance and success rate will both improve.

Example: Over the last two months, you have participated actively in weekly staff meetings. You have raised several points and swayed others to your point of view about half the time. You study those instances and compare them to the times your point of view did not prevail. The common thread, you discover, relates to your own preparation level. The better prepared, the more frequently your recommendations were taken.

DIFFERING AGENDAS

Never assume that you and your fellow attendees have identical agendas. And recognize that the printed agenda you receive is only a rough guideline. In reality, all meeting attendees have an unspoken agenda of their own. And that will determine their opinions, points of view, and responses to everything you say.

This presents a problem of preparation. It may prove useless to prepare yourself for a meeting based strictly on the agenda items you are told will be covered. In fact, the meeting might take a direction completely different from the one you expected, and your presentation might never have a chance.

Before you attend a meeting, you must first understand one important point: *The real purpose of the meeting is often unspoken and will not appear on a written page.*

If you measure success in terms of the influence you have in your organization, meetings can be very frustrating. To succeed in any organizational culture, you must be able to evaluate and understand the unspoken realities that motivate people. The accuracy of your perceptions may well determine how well you are able to implement anything.

Example: You attend a meeting prepared to discuss upcoming budgeting procedures, which is the single agenda item. However, you never get a chance to discuss the procedural ideas you have. As it turns out, the meeting time is devoted to a debate concerning responsibility and budget authority. One group believes the accounting department should prepare the entire budget, and another thinks it should be decentralized. The detailed recommendations you prepared never come up.

This reality is not a negative force; it is merely a fact of life in any organization. The better you understand what really motivates others, and the more you know about how things really work in your company, the greater your success will be in exercising influence. And meetings are the corporation's forum for demonstrating influence and—to a degree—political awareness. In the example above, you could have prepared for the meeting by thinking about your position on the issue that did come up, and preparing a compromise position that might have solved the problem to everyone's satisfaction.

Constantly be aware of the different points of view that others hold, notably as they affect your own participation in meetings. Never attempt to present your case in isolation, no matter how much sense it makes. As an attendee, you might not understand what is really going to occur in a meeting, unless you understand the real issues at work. Even though the decision makers in your company will be guided by the bottom line, that is not enough. You must also know how to present your case with the differing agendas of other attendees in mind.

Being aware that each person comes to a meeting with his or her own agenda, follow these guidelines (see Figure 8-2):

1. *Never present just one side.* The best argument you can make is one that raises conflicting points of view and then shows how your solution will work.

2. *Always expect disagreement.* It is safe to assume that others will disagree with you, whether they say so or not. This is true for several reasons. First, if you propose a change, you must accept the fact that people always resist new ideas. Second, other attendees may feel threatened by conflict itself, even when your motive is not personal. And third, meetings are perceived by many as places to create a debate, no matter what issues are raised. And finally, meeting topics may bring out honest disagreements.

3. *Deal with conflict calmly.* Avoid making arguments that do not address company issues directly. For the executive who is aware of a broad number of concerns, hearing inappropriate arguments may be an irritating but constant experience. For example, when you are faced with conflict in a meeting, always defend your position with arguments concerning profits, efficiency, and progress of work tasks.

Figure 8-2. Presentation guidelines.

1. Never present just one side.

2. Always expect disagreement.

3. Deal with conflict calmly.

4. Confront issues and not people.

5. Work around closed minds.

4. *Confront issues and not people.* In debating an issue, never make it personal (even when the other side does). Stay with the issues. When meetings degenerate into personality struggles, nothing can be achieved.

5. *Work around closed minds.* Any time you suggest change, you will surely hear one of two arguments: "But we've never done it that way," or "It's not in the budget." These are the most common responses to any new idea. The tendency is to argue with tradition, which places you in a weak position. Don't attempt to confront these arguments directly. Instead, respond with the question "If it wasn't for that one point, would you have a problem with this idea?"

THE IMPORTANT PREMEETING

A lot of energy that goes into the strategy of meetings could be eliminated with a little communication. When an attendee spends time trying to outguess someone else, that's not really preparation at all. It might prove more effective simply to meet with other attendees before the larger meeting takes place.

Example: You plan to suggest a revision in procedures at an upcoming management meeting. Your suggestion will change the way that your department operates and will also affect two other departments directly. You have prepared a report that demonstrates cost savings from your ideas. You meet with the managers of the other departments and explain your ideas to them, asking, "What positive and negative consequences do you see coming from this idea? How can I modify my proposal so that it addresses your concerns?"

It's a courtesy to consult with other managers who will be affected by your proposal. However, taking this step is no guarantee that they will agree to your suggestion. There are several possible results:

1. *Complete disagreement.* If another department's manager has a problem with your idea, get the specifics. You might discover that there are issues you did not consider. If the savings in your department are offset by increased costs in another, the idea might not be as sound as

you thought. Get as much information as you can from others, and be willing to back down if they prove to you that, overall, your idea is not practical.

If you are convinced that your idea has merit, even when someone else does not agree with you, conclude your discussion by saying, "I wanted to let you know ahead of time what I'm planning to propose, so that you wouldn't be taken by surprise in the meeting."

2. *Agreement with qualifications.* Other managers might agree that your idea is a good one; however, other points might need to be considered. For example, an idea that makes your department operate more efficiently could rob another department of information it needs. The result: It will cost more to replace what you propose to take away. This situation presents an opportunity to make your idea more forceful. Propose to the other manager that your proposal be revised with his concerns in mind and then presented as a joint recommendation.

3. *Acceptance.* When another department manager agrees that you have a good idea and further states that he will not create any problems for you, you have gained the best advantage possible going into the meeting: an ally. You can now expand your case by saying that another manager has reviewed the idea and that it will not create any problems for him. As long as you have addressed the issues of concern to the decision makers—profits, efficiency, and procedures—you have a much better chance of gaining approval with this alliance.

You might be tempted to avoid premeetings with others, in the belief that your interests will not be served. If another manager does not approve of your proposal, the premeeting gives him time to prepare an opposing argument. But keep these points in mind:

1. *Being right is your best asset.* If your idea is a good one and you present it clearly, not even a good counterargument can refute it. Too much energy is put into defending an obvious position when there is no need. Present your case and your proof, and don't say any more than you need to say to make your point.

2. *Dissent can help your case.* Once you know why someone else does not like your idea, you know how to build that into your presentation. Plan to raise the point and refute it.

3. *Conflict is no threat to thoughtful ideas.* If you do not want interaction, then your ideas should be presented directly to the decision maker and not raised in a meeting setting. Since meetings are intended as the place to make informed decisions, you lose nothing by explaining ideas to others in advance.

4. *Weak positions are self-destructive.* You need to fear disclosing your plans in advance only when you know they are not sound. Deal with weak points in your proposal before you make a presentation. If you cannot, then reevaluate your entire proposal, and ask yourself whether it is truly sound.

The day may come when you make an honest effort to communicate with someone in advance of a meeting, only to have it backfire. For example, a manager who disagrees with your proposal goes around to others and builds an alliance in opposition to your proposal. As the result of planned consensus, your idea is rejected.

If that occurs, keep in mind that communication is a positive exercise, but it contains dangers. Once you know who not to trust, you will proceed with caution the next time around. Don't avoid communication and all of its positive attributes just to protect yourself against an occasional setback. Instead, proceed ethically and honestly and be willing to live with the risk of losing an argument now and then.

LINING UP SUPPORT

The political forces at work in your company can be used in very positive, constructive ways. Remembering that other people can be expected to resist change, you might need to organize a lot of support before your meeting—even when your ideas make perfect sense. And this can be achieved in an honest manner involving no conspiracy, but a sincere effort to make meetings work well.

Communicating with other people beforehand helps eliminate surprises during a meeting. Nobody likes to be taken off guard, and you will gain influence by disclosing your intentions to others in advance. When you give other people the chance to prepare, they cannot justify the argument for putting off a decision. And when conflicting points of view are aired before the meeting, your presentation can only be improved.

Another benefit of creating a dialogue is that you might identify your subject as being inappropriate for the meeting. To avoid having your judgment questioned by others, determine in advance whether the meeting you will attend is the appropriate place to raise your points.

Example: You plan to suggest a change in procedures during an upcoming meeting. You discuss your plan with another manager, who responds, "I don't think this meeting is the right place to raise this point."

A meeting could be inappropriate to your purposes for several reasons:

1. *Wrong agenda.* If a meeting is structured to discuss a limited range of topics in a short time span, and your idea is not on the agenda, it will never be well received.

Example: You attend a meeting where the agenda calls for a discussion of the coming year's marketing plan. You want to present ideas for improving the internal marketing tracking system, but you realize that this meeting is not the place to raise that issue.

2. *Consideration of the meeting leader.* When an idea is proposed as a new agenda item, it could be taken as an insult to a meeting leader. Be sensitive to the cultural realities of meetings. Some are designed as truly interactive gatherings; others serve as the private theater for one person. Don't attempt to present an idea when the leader will not appreciate it. Wait for a better opportunity.

Example: The leader has a specific agenda in mind for a manager's meeting and always concludes by asking for any comments or suggestions. At that point, attempting to present your plan could be seen as stealing the limelight.

3. *Nature of the issue.* Some problems, proposals, and solutions should never be discussed in a group meeting. Always ask yourself whether the other attendees have a need to know. Can they contribute to solutions? Will presenting these facts embarrass or offend anyone?

Example: When you have a problem with an employee and want to discuss it, wait until you can meet with your supervisor privately. Avoid discussing payroll information in meetings. Do not bring up issues that might prove embarrassing to the organization.

ANTICIPATING CONFLICTS

Your perception of a meeting's purpose and value will determine what you hope to achieve with premeetings. The meeting can serve as the place to bring up issues and to have them discussed; but a discussion without a decision and follow-up action is preliminary at best. More often than not, discussions result in nothing.

A second perception is that the meeting serves as the place to make *final* decisions. This is not the same as consensus. If the decision makers in your company try to please everyone, then no one is satisfied and, more to the point, nothing will get done. In order for management to make the right decision, agreement and consensus are not requirements. However, the meeting does allow everyone the chance to voice opinions and to offer information. Through this process, final decisions are much easier to arrive at and put into action.

Anyone who has been through the problem-solving process knows that important issues are not always resolved quickly or easily. When a number of different people are affected by the decision, many points of view and other issues—budgets and personnel, for example—must be considered, in addition to what appears the "best" decision in a given case. Because some issues are especially complicated, a single meeting often proves inconclusive, with important decisions delayed until a later date.

You can do a lot to make meetings work more efficiently. Recognizing that a decision rarely involves a single dimension, you can eliminate much conflict before the question comes before the meeting.

Example: You want to suggest that the budgeting process now in use should be revised. You have a number of specific ideas, all of which you believe can be put into effect during the upcoming year-end budget exercise. You are aware that merely presenting your proposal would create a lot of discussion and distract the meeting away from the critical question "Should we adopt a different procedure for budgeting?"

Knowing that a number of department heads have strong opinions on this subject, you approach each one and discuss your proposal. In those instances where a manager has different ideas, you are able to arrive at agreement on how some things should be handled. You also listen to differing ideas about the budgeting process.

By the time you're ready to give your report, you are able to summarize the conflicts as part of your presentation. This will discourage unnecessary dialogue that would consume time and discourage a final solution.

By airing the issues in advance of the meeting, you will provide the opportunity to get down to business. The decision makers will not have to listen to expanded and often unproductive versions of the same argument, nor to arguments against your ideas. Once you have summarized all of that, any expanded and repetitive discussion will be unnecessary.

By limiting the need for discussion, you allow the decision makers to consider the issue in a clarified form. And when you enrich your presentation by summing up the arguments for and against your idea, you save everyone in attendance a lot of time and energy.

EXPRESSING YOUR IDEAS

Because no one likes surprises at meetings, the best way to become an influential force is to clearly communicate with everyone involved—well before the meeting itself—when you have an idea you would like to discuss.

The one step most often overlooked by meeting attendees is to approach the leader and ask that their topic be added to the agenda. A meeting often ends up as a competition between attendees, who are trying to raise issues on their own agendas. In this case, the intended agenda of the meeting must suffer. As an alternative, a meeting can be an organized, productive exercise in management and action if all attendees respect the agenda and the meeting's time constraints.

Besides communicating items on your own agenda so that they

become incorporated into the meeting's formal one, also prepare your-self by determining how an issue affects your department, the organiza-tion, and you. Address each issue by asking these questions:

1. *How does this affect my department?* If an issue does not affect your department directly, allow other attendees to speak. Contribute your thoughts only if asked, or only if you are able to make an observation that you think will help resolve a problem.

If there is a direct effect, you must speak up and explain the issues to the other attendees. If you don't take advantage of the opportunity presented at a meeting, then attendance is useless.

2. *What is the effect on the organization?* How does a decision, for or against an idea, affect profits? The issue must be raised at every point of conflict, since the organization will ultimately make a decision on that basis.

In addition, you must question the effects on personnel, efficiency, and productivity. Some ideas might seem at first to offer practical solutions; but in review, the impact on nonfinancial conditions might not be worth the trouble.

3. *What is the effect on me?* Everyone has a point of view that is guided at least in part by the desire for self-preservation. Certainly a manager will react strongly when he hears a proposal by someone else to close his department. However, even less drastic proposals and solu-tions could have serious effects on your own career. When you speak up to offer a different point of view, be sure you address the issues from the organization's point of view. Avoid airing your personal priorities, even when they are on the top of your list. That only weakens your argument.

Once you know the best way to prepare for a meeting, you are ready to offer ideas of value to the organization and to other attendees. At this point you might face a new threat. For many, speaking out at a meeting is an intimidating and frightening experience. Because of this natural fear, many talented people remain mute rather than taking risks.

When you do speak out, you expose yourself to criticism from others, and no one wants to be questioned in public. The next chapter explains how to prepare for participation with this problem in mind.

WORK PROJECT

1. You plan to propose a major change in procedures at an upcoming meeting. Explain how you can develop proof that your idea will improve profits; and tell how you can anticipate and deal with conflicts that might arise in response.

2. List two guidelines for making a presentation during a meeting, and state how these help you to win a positive decision.

3. Give two reasons for arranging a premeeting with other managers who will attend a meeting with you. Explain how the premeeting will help you to present your ideas better.

9

Defining Attendee Participation

Try skipping a meeting if you want to find out how important it is.

—Robert Townsend

"Most of the meetings we hold are a complete waste of time," one executive admitted to another. "I'd like to figure out a way to make them more productive."

"We've had the same problem in our division," the other replied. "In fact, a few of us are getting together after lunch to discuss it. Would you like to sit in?"

A rewarding meeting is one in which each attendee is given the freedom to express ideas and, at least occasionally, to win approval for a proposal. Meetings are truly dynamic when anyone who attends has the chance to improve the system.

People like meetings. They are not work sessions, but sessions to plan work, to gain support and endorsement of ideas, and to validate approaches to problems. When meetings are organized and run properly, they can be the most productive use of time in your company, if only to define the work that must follow. You can make the most of a positive meeting situation. The experience of progressing in a meeting is a rewarding one that will improve your self-esteem as well as your effectiveness. Raise your voice when you have a good idea, and express your opinions. Question. And look for ways to improve the internal operation.

The quality of meetings can be improved by suggestions from attendees. If you try to change the structure and content of meetings and then continue attending, you will make a difference, no matter what rank you hold. Strive to define how you can most effectively participate and play a positive role.

FEAR OF SPEAKING OUT

It is much easier to *say* you can speak up than to actually take a stand, especially a stand that will not be well received by others. As everyone involved in business already knows, people who speak out expose themselves to risk. You have to conquer two fears before you will be able to make a difference in how meetings are conducted:

1. *Fear of conflict.* When you state a position that goes against the majority, you are immediately at risk. This exposure could affect your career. But as long as you are prepared to support your position with facts, you're on solid ground.

Example: You question the validity of continuing to prepare budgets in the accounting department and make a case for decentralized preparation. Several other attendees disagree strongly. You refer to past budgets as proof that their value is limited—because managers are held responsible for overruns in their departments, but have no say in the budgets they must live with.

2. *Fear of attention.* This is the same fear that prevents many people from speaking in public. Few of us are comfortable with the idea of standing up and speaking.

Example: You have an idea you believe will solve an ongoing problem. But you hesitate during a meeting, because you do not want to draw attention to yourself. You speak to your supervisor away from the meeting, and he instructs you to organize a report and present it at the next meeting. Even though you are uncomfortable with the assignment, you proceed. Your idea is well received and your recommendations are approved.

Fearing conflict is natural in most corporations because we can never be certain that top managers really want to hear opposing viewpoints. We fear that they want uniformity and consensus, and speaking out creates a problem.

Fearing attention is equally deadly. If you have listened to other managers and executives speak at meetings, you already know that most people present views that go along with the beliefs that drive your organization.

It's much easier to stay "in line" with what we perceive as a safe posture. Ask yourself, "What is the real risk of taking a stand?" If your motives are to improve productivity, streamline a procedure, reduce expenses, and increase profits, why not express your ideas in those terms?

Whenever you attend a meeting, look for opportunities to participate, and don't settle for mere audience status. To take this idea and put it into action, focus your attention on definition. Take these steps:

1. *Define participation.* For every meeting you're asked to attend, ask the question "How will I participate?" If you're told that you need only to be there, ask the reason. Make your case based on the belief that there's a valid purpose for you to go to a meeting only when you contribute something of value.

Example: You are invited to a meeting later this week and ask, "What would you like me to prepare for the session?" The vice-president who will lead the meeting tells you not to worry about it; just show up. You answer that you want to participate in the best way possible and would like to see an agenda. The vice-president is surprised, but recognizes your argument as a positive trait.

2. *Be prepared to offer an opinion.* Back up your position by preparing facts, and attend the meeting prepared to argue your case. Even if the opportunity to speak out does not come up, you will at least know you're well prepared.

Example: Your supervisor was very impressed at last week's staff meeting. When the subject of hiring more employees came up, the accountant insisted that the budget was full and no new people could be brought on board this year. But you disagreed. You presented facts proving that by hiring two new people in your division, you could eliminate overhead and do away with delays in processing. The savings, your figures proved, would exceed the cost of payroll. The president approved your recommendation.

3. *Use the chain of command.* One of the frustrating aspects of all communication is the tendency to approach problems in vague terms. Use the chain of command in meetings to identify where responsibility lies. And then add to the value of discussions by helping the group define that responsibility.

Example: An executive gathers a number of managers together to talk about long-term marketing plans. The question on the table is "How do we decide how to finance an expansion program?" One manager suggests that, while everyone there can contribute to the discussion, the ultimate decision must be made on the executive level.

With these strategies, you're not flying in the face of accepted procedures, but only making your best case for validity.

THE FREEDOM TO SPEAK OUT

The next question to deal with is whether or not you can speak out freely. In some meetings the design allows only one individual to speak, while everyone else is relegated to the position of passive audience member.

This situation must be expected to arise in some meetings. The only way you can help to improve the situation is to ask *how* you can participate. Look for a way that you can make a contribution, even a minor one. Don't passively accept the idea of going to a meeting without bringing knowledge or information of value. If these ideas do not work, you might have to simply accept the fact that some meeting leaders don't really understand the purpose of a meeting.

The freedom to speak out exists on many levels. The meeting—especially the one where you are not given that freedom—is the least effective forum of all. Seek outlets for the free expression of opinion. All employees want to voice an opinion and have it respected, and this is possible only when their ideas are listened to and, when they're good, acted on. Consider these alternative outlets:

1. *Your immediate supervisor.* No one has as much direct influence on your career as your boss does. You can deal with a supervisor on a one-to-one basis, so that the complex intrigues and complications of gathering several people together are not a factor. And when you have a good idea, it can be decided on less formally. This removes many of the cultural conflicts that might prevent meetings from being constructive.

A supervisor can also protect you when your point of view is right but unpopular. One advantage of the chain of command, when properly used, is that you cannot be expected to take risks that your boss should take. If you have a good idea, but others disagree with it, include your supervisor. Let the boss take any heat from others.

2. *Fellow managers.* The lower the number of people in a meeting, the better the communication level, and the better the chance for positive action. Thus, when you have a point of view you believe will create controversy, speak with other managers. Explain your position and gather allies to your cause.

3. *Adversaries.* You may find yourself in a position of making a case when other managers disagree with you. (In the "grapevine" approach, an individual speaks to everyone about the problem, *except* the adversary.)

Try this approach: Meet directly with the adversary and talk about your points of view. You might learn a great deal about *why* the other manager opposes your ideas, and as a result, you could change your mind as well. Or you might be able to convince others that your idea is not as threatening as they thought.

Some people will say it is naïve to think that you can approach an adversary and change his or her mind. However, most of the misunderstandings that arise in corporations (or in government, families, or any other cultural setting) exist because no one tried to talk. When you find yourself in conflict with someone, the first step should be to get together and talk. Even if you cannot come to an agreement or a compromise, you will at least define the problem completely and better understand a different point of view.

Never overlook the fact that the freedom to speak extends beyond the meeting. Don't use meetings as the only place to air your views, when you should be speaking directly with someone else—a supervisor, a fellow manager, or even with someone who has taken the position of an enemy.

THE SUMMARIZED PRESENTATION

Even when the leadership of a meeting is enlightened enough to allow you to participate in a valuable way, you must still bear the responsibility for taking action. It is not enough that you have the opportunity; you must also react within the context you are provided.

In a busy agenda, and with a limited timetable, meetings should move along quickly. The best meetings deal with the important issues and not the details. For you as a participating attendee, this means you must carefully choose the statements you make and the facts you present.

Example: You attend a meeting to present a lengthy and complex report. In the five minutes you're given to make your presentation, what will you say?

An effective way to present a lot of material in a short period of time is to concentrate on the highlights. Start with your major conclusions and recommendations, support those final conclusions with the major facts you used, and then wrap up by referring to the supporting documentation in your report.

Guidelines for meeting presentations serve as excellent guidelines for preparing reports. Every report should summarize the essential information on the first page and report conclusions, recommendations, proposed action, and deadlines. If your report includes the valuable summary page, your verbal presentation in a meeting should not be difficult.

One manager took this approach: She began by explaining the

purpose of the report in the context of the problem being examined. This segment was very brief, limited to two or three precise statements. Next, she explained the approach taken in analyzing and researching the defined problem. This included historical data, interviews, use of material from other departments, and guidelines from management. Third, she stated that the details supporting major conclusions could be found in the body of the report. Fourth, she explained the major conclusions drawn. And finally, she listed her recommendations for action, including responsibility and deadlines.

This is a variation of the steps suggested above. Depending on the nature of a report, it might be more effective to preface your conclusions with explanations. In other cases your communication will be improved by going right to the bottom line.

The appropriate variation of this presentation format will always lead to discussion by the meeting attendees. However, the important point is that the essence of the report is communicated clearly and directly. If anyone challenges your assumptions or the conclusions you draw, support is easily located within the report itself.

The same approach can be used for communicating anything during a meeting, short of a formal report. Before you attend, prepare an outline of agenda items that affect you and your department. Clarify your position by writing out the five steps listed in Figure 9-1.

Example: During a general meeting, a discussion takes place concerning the problems of getting projects completed in time. One manager makes a brief statement:

> I believe the problem is that deadlines are not always specific, and that once an assignment is given there is no set procedure for following up. (Defined problem)
> We've overcome this problem in our division by monitoring projects as they proceed, and identifying trouble spots. (Methods)
> In fact, we wrote up a report of our findings, which I'll make available to anyone who's interested. (Information sources)
> We concluded that projects will be completed on time only when the manager checks progress on a regular basis. (Conclusion)
> I recommend that we consider installing a similar procedure for all departments, and that each manager should be ready to

Figure 9-1. Presentation phases.

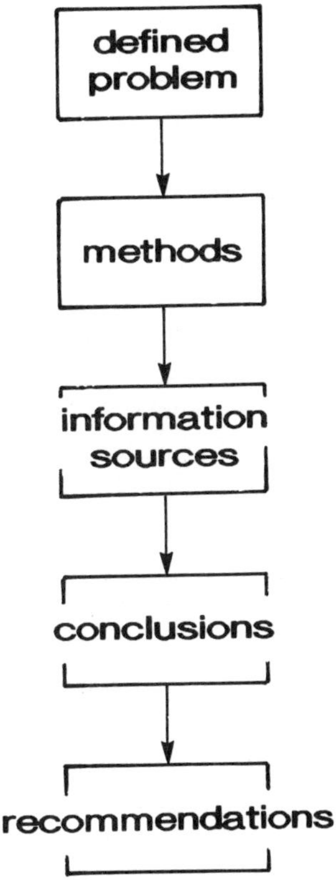

proceed with a follow-up system one month from today. (Recommendations, including responsibility, action, and deadline)

Without a specific recommendation based on hard facts or evidence, a meeting's discussions might ramble on in generalities without any practical results. But when one attendee explains how he or she solved a similar problem, or just observes the problem from one point of view and states the obvious solution, the meeting becomes worthwhile and productive for all attendees.

DEBATE ETIQUETTE

Even if you approach problems by proposing solutions and then asking for specific answers, you might still create a conflict. Others sharing similar rank may resent the fact that you're vocalizing a response commitment and trying to get exact answers. And those who outrank you might resist the idea that a subordinate wants answers to the issues raised.

A good deal of the action that *should* come from meetings is the leader's responsibility. But because the quality of leaders does vary, you cannot always depend on the leader to take the meeting on an action track.

As long as you're asked to attend a meeting, you have the right—and the responsibility—to do everything in your power to create positive results. You can defend your actions by responding in one of many ways. For example:

- I would never presume to give you an assignment. I only want to ensure, on behalf of everyone here, that our agreed course of action will go into effect.
- Please don't misunderstand my motives. I'm only interested in a solution.
- I apologize if my persistence is offensive. But I thought we all agreed on the direction to take. I'm only trying to find out how and when the work is going to be done.

Persistence, no matter how well motivated and no matter how diplomatically worded, will create conflict and might be a threat to others in the meeting—especially when your persistence involves their department. Never argue over your "right" to ask important questions; always refer to the committee's purpose at large, and if you must defend your position, do so in the context of responsibility, not right or wrong. Don't allow the discussion to degenerate into a power struggle, because that's not what participation is all about.

Your participation during the meeting must be tempered with diplomacy. If you want to have a voice in the affairs of your company, you will have to be sensitive to the attitudes and perceptions of others.

ACTION STEPS FOR ATTENDEES

Follow these guidelines when you attend meetings:

1. *Identify the risks in taking a position and speaking out.* Once you identify the real risk, you will have an idea of how strongly to speak out.

2. *Always attempt to define participation, and when someone asks you to attend a meeting, ask what is expected from you.* Look for a way that you can make a positive contribution.

3. *While listening to discussions, seek ways to arrive at logical and worthwhile decisions and conclusions.* Suggest your ideas to the group.

4. *Don't overlook the obvious outlets for your ideas, beyond the meeting forum.* Discuss your ideas with your supervisor, fellow managers, and even with adversaries.

5. *When you make presentations during meetings, speak as briefly as possible.* Give only the highlights and leave details to the printed document. This will hold the interest of other attendees and enable you to get right to the point.

6. *Remember that your group needs to know the three elements of action: who, what, and when.* *Who* will act, *what* will be done, and *when* will the job be completed?

7. *Always employ tact when forwarding questions designed to define solutions.* The leader should lead the discussion, but might fail to do so; however, when you take over and ask, you could alienate the leader unintentionally.

WORK PROJECT

1. Explain two of the three points that define meetings, and discuss the ways that these points help you to improve your level of participation.

2. Explain the five-step presentation method and how it helps you summarize complex information briefly.

10

Attendees:
After the Meeting

There is something about a bureaucracy that does not like a poem.

—Gore Vidal

"We've made big improvements in our procedures," the vice-president boasted. "The average manager's time spent in meetings has been reduced from 30 minutes per day, down to 15."

One manager meekly observed, "That's true. But now most of us are also attending twice as many meetings as before."

As a meeting attendee, you should know what your responsibility is after the meeting has ended. One way to test the validity of the meetings you attend is to ask yourself, "What assignments was I given, and how should I now respond?"

If you cannot identify a precise answer to this test, then you should question what value was derived from the meeting. Others might have received benefits; in fact, a meeting can be a useful experience for some attendees, while others come away with little or nothing of value.

In this chapter we will provide guidelines for actions attendees should take in response to what was decided during a meeting, how to participate in solutions that were agreed on, and how a meeting affects your point of view about an issue.

THE PROBLEM OF BUREAUCRACY

As companies expand, there must exist a constant struggle between action and bureaucracy. The human desire for order, even when intended for positive reasons, can become lost in the internal mechanisms aimed at organizing and tracking events. As long as order is achieved, a system is worthwhile; but when the paperwork becomes more important than the work itself, the result is a bureaucracy. And that can stifle progress, actually preventing the very actions you want to take in response to assignments.

This situation presents a challenge to anyone who wants to respond with action after a meeting. We must remember that the meeting itself is a group effort and thrives well as long as individuals are allowed to proceed with their work. Group thinking can be of great value in the meeting; but once the group is disbanded, the individual must be able to take over.

Example: During a staff meeting, the vice-president stated that a report should be prepared, a study of the costs involved in installing an improved telephone system. The purpose, as you understood it, was to decide whether the investment would pay off in future savings and efficiency. In response, you begin work on a report. You call many phone service companies, compare prices and systems, and speak with other managers. However, you run into a problem whenever you approach others who were at the meeting. One manager says, "Why are you doing this work? I thought it was supposed to be a group effort."

Unless a specific assignment has been given to you to proceed with action, you might find resistance along the way. Ironically, there might be no such thing as a "group effort," and you might discover instead that real action occurs only when individuals take the initiative.

Why do people resist positive action? Part of the reason is fear of taking a chance. Others may believe that by responding you are taking risks. Somehow, that is transferred into the spirit of *not* cooperating. To question a well-motivated, appropriate response is one form of resisting change. Others perceive your positive responses as a threat to them, even when your actions are taken independently.

Whenever you are up against bureaucratic thinking, use these strategies (see Figure 10-1):

1. *Get a specific assignment.* Meetings sometimes conclude without a clear decision being made. If you think it is appropriate to take action directly, you should volunteer during the meeting and ask for a clear, specific assignment from the group leader.

If, after the meeting, you realize that you did not receive a specific assignment, it's not too late. Approach your supervisor or the individual who is in charge of the project, and ask for clarification. Then, when you are questioned by others as you proceed, you can respond that you have been given the direct assignment.

Figure 10-1. Strategies: dealing with a bureaucracy.

1. Get a specific assignment.

2. Take the team approach.

3. Confront resistance.

4. Write a memo.

5. Submit an incomplete report.

6. Get your facts elsewhere.

2. *Take the team approach.* Teamwork can mean many things. Most people think of it as several individuals working together to achieve a common and well-defined goal. But a team can function toward that purpose only if the goals are, in fact, specifically defined and understood. It's frustrating to discover that other members of the team perceive the problem and likely solutions differently than you do.

To take the team approach, you must first determine that everyone in your meeting understands and agrees on what problem must be solved. This first step might take more time than the solution itself. The second phase is to decide how each team member will participate. You do not need consensus to make a team work. Consensus is rarely possible. But in an effective team, individuals will be willing to compromise as long as they are given the chance to state their point of view. Finally, a solution can proceed when team members accept assignments that contribute to the solution, under the coordination of a person holding primary responsibility. That could be the meeting leader or an attendee who accepts the assignment.

3. *Confront resistance.* One of the most frustrating experiences an honestly motivated person can have is running into resistance where it is not justified or fair.

Example: A manager was given a project task by the president of the company during a meeting. However, when the manager approached other department heads, some made it quite clear that they would not cooperate with the project.

When you experience this unpleasant form of resistance, some face-to-face discussion might help. But if the other person is determined to resist, there really is little you can do directly. There is not much point in confronting the person; however, you can take several steps to confront resistance.

We must recognize that resistance occurs because people feel left out. If no team exists, you cannot expect others to cheerfully cooperate in helping you to achieve *your* goals—especially if they believe they have been excluded from the decision. Another cause of resistance is the sense that an action threatens someone's security.

These are difficult issues to confront, because even in a business setting they become highly personal and sensitive. Out-and-out resistance may be hostile and confrontative, making it difficult for you to even create a preliminary dialogue of any value.

First, use your supervisor's help. Let someone higher up on the chain of command deal with the problem, even if it means going to someone else's boss on your behalf.

A second idea is to explain what you're doing from a different point of view. It could be that the other manager perceived your assignment as a power play or as an action that, in some way, was threatening. Explain what you're doing from your point of view, and then ask the other person for his own impressions. That might open the door to a mutually useful dialogue.

4. *Write a memo.* Human interaction—in a large meeting or even during a one-to-one discussion—is likely to be full of misunderstandings. Verbal communication is a difficult art. Thus, your position might be better stated in writing than in person. With a memo you can methodically explain the reasoning behind a decision; you can present major points from several points of view; and you can proceed through your explanation without argument, interruption, or misunderstandings.

Use the memo to set up the project you're trying to complete. Explain what you're going to do and what the results will be. State exactly what help you need, when you need it, and in what format. And then make a specific request for help. Also end the memo by asking for a response. You want to hear back from the other people, even if they only tell you that they will *not* help you.

Always follow up on a memo with a telephone call or visit. Once the other people have had a chance to read your memo, go to them and ask for a response. If they want to resist helping, chances are good they will simply fail to respond to your memo. In that case your best move is to follow up in person.

5. *Submit an incomplete report.* You can do all you can to get help from others and simply be unable to convince them to take part. In that case you have a choice: Either delay completion of the entire report, or work around the uncooperative people.

It will not always be possible to come to a complete conclusion in your assignment without help from others. But whenever you can prepare a report without help, leave out the segments of your report that rest with other people and work around it. If necessary, estimate or assume as an alternative to delay.

6. *Get your facts elsewhere.* When someone refuses to help you gather needed information for your assignment, you must be prepared to find your own facts. Look elsewhere, put in extra time if necessary, and develop your own set of assumptions.

One of the best ways to make the point that no one is indispensable is to establish that you're able to proceed even without the participation of others. This remains unspoken, of course; but it's an effective way to achieve the purposes of your assignment *and* prove that no people in the organization have so much control that your job cannot be done without them.

CREATING ACTION AND RESPONSE

Getting results from managers who resist and fear change, or from any bureaucratic structure, is quite difficult. You can either put a lot of effort into asking for a response or find answers on your own. And if the other people simply refuse to work with you, then you're on your own.

These problems exist, to a degree, in most organizations. But even within the company that includes a good deal of bureaucracy, most people are fairly easy to work with and will respond to you if your requests are presented in the right manner.

You will be more likely to receive a favorable response when you apply these guidelines (see Figure 10-2):

1. *Be aware of organizational protocol.* If your request for help should go through a supervisory chain of command, don't bypass it. Respect the formality of that chain. One of the reasons it exists is to prevent the types of misunderstandings and antagonisms that will prevent you from achieving your assignment goals.

2. *Phrase your request carefully.* Be aware that individuals might feel offended by even the most carefully worded request. If you enter someone else's department and are perceived to be demanding help— that is, if the other person believes you are giving *her* an assignment— you could be headed for trouble. Be aware that fellow employees may be overly sensitive to being asked for help from outside of their depart-

Figure 10-2. Asking for help.

1. **Be aware of organizational protocol.**

2. **Phrase your request carefully.**

3. **Ask for suggestions.**

4. **Be sensitive to time restraints.**

5. **Be aware of resource problems.**

6. **Apply meeting standards.**

7. **Follow up with a memo.**

ments. Even what you consider a friendly question could be mistaken for an attempt to exert power, demand help, or bypass the proper procedures.

3. *Ask for suggestions.* The best way to avoid being misunderstood is to ask *indirectly* for the specific information you want. Take a few moments and explain the background: the assignment you have been given, the problem you're trying to solve, and the approach you plan to take. Then ask the other person for suggestions she might offer.

A sincere request is flattering as well as appropriate. Not only are you likely to receive the assistance you ask for, you might just get ideas or points of view you hadn't even considered. After asking for suggestions, you should then mention the specific form of help you had in mind.

4. *Be sensitive to time restraints.* Never place an unreasonable demand on someone else. Immediate response from another department is not always possible, and asking for it places a lot of pressure on the other person. It may also add to the feeling that you're trying to exercise power rather than simply making a request.

If you do need something right away, explain your deadline and ask whether it will create a problem. If it does, take all the steps you can to facilitate the other person's schedule, even if that means asking for an extension on the report.

5. *Be aware of resource problems.* Another point you must remember is that the other department manager had deadlines and tasks to perform in addition to the task you need help with. Most managers believe they're understaffed and overworked; when you approach them and impose yet another task, their own departmental situation could present a serious problem in priorities.

If necessary, offer to loan employees from your department, especially when the help you're requesting will mean a good deal of research or file retrieval.

6. *Apply meeting standards.* Don't overlook the fact that when you speak with the manager of another department you're in a meeting. Apply the standards that make all meetings successful. Define your problem and the proposed solution, lay out your agenda, and specify the deadline.

7. *Follow up with a memo.* To ensure that your communication with another person was clear, summarize the discussion in a memo. If any differing perceptions arise after your meeting, a concise and clear memo will certainly bring them out.

Your memo should summarize the discussion as you understand it, including a list of the points each of you agreed on. Then the other person has the chance to respond and clarify any points of disagreement.

RESPONDING TO ASSIGNMENTS

Whether you need to access resources outside of your department or complete an assignment on your own, it is essential that you respond appropriately. If meetings are to serve as a valid forum for action, then you will have to formulate a response.

A meeting—properly used—enables you to clarify the tasks you are expected to perform, to perfect the definition phase of accepting an assignment, and to perform your entire job better. If meetings in your company are structured to create a climate in which this is possible, then the challenge of accomplishing what you set out to do will be much easier.

How can you perform above average in your company? The answer is fundamental. Simply clarify an assignment in the meeting, commit yourself to completing the task by a specified deadline, and then come through.

If you are able to complete that essential chain of events, you will succeed. However, also be aware that in the course of attempting to utilize meetings for a constructive purpose, you might have a formidable task. Before discussing your response, it is necessary to identify the problem that every company meeting presents.

The inexperienced manager who has learned all about meetings from a textbook but has never attended a real one does not realize what meetings are all about. But the seasoned manager already knows that in order to put the concept to work—just to reach the point of having a specific assignment to which to respond—you must first struggle with the reality of meetings.

Getting a group of people together in a room and expecting them to work well together is, by itself, quite a challenge. Each individual perceives in a highly personal manner. The same message creates a different response and perception from each peson. So what you consider an obvious and straightforward task might be disruptive and complex to the person sitting next to you. This is the ongoing and never-ending communications problem that everyone must confront when dealing with other people.

Being aware of this reality will solve a problem that every meeting attendee faces. If you are not aware of the perception differences going on during the meeting, then you cannot devise a constructive way to achieve the results you expect. To simply believe that everyone in attendance wants the same things you want will prevent you from getting the definition and action decisions you have a right to expect.

You might find that, rather than getting to the point where you can respond to an assignment, the problems never come up at all. You are far from powerless in creating a meeting environment that's constructive rather than political. Be vocal. Ask for definition, and respect points of view different from your own. In looking for decisions and action, remember that the way you perceive a problem is not necessarily the only way.

Then, and only then, can you expect to have a productive meeting, in which you and the other attendees achieve anything of value. The next step is to develop the means for response to assignments. Don't put off the task, but become involved as soon as the meeting is through. Schedule your actions so that you will have ample time to meet your deadline.

IMMEDIATE RESPONSE

When you respond quickly, that *should* be perceived as a positive trait, or, as it is often vaguely expressed, the sign of a "good" attitude. Unfortunately, quick response is often viewed as a definite negative.

Example: You are given the assignment of preparing a report within three days. Two days later the report is complete, so you distribute it. The response from some recipients is to question the validity of the report, since it was completed *too* quickly. Meeting a deadline is exceptional enough; people may even think that being a day or two late is acceptable. But being *early* is unheard of.

This is true for many reasons. Some fellow employees might think that you are trying to make them look less efficient—grandstanding to gain points with the boss. Others will feel directly threatened by a too-fast response, perhaps because they are not able to complete similar assignments at once.

Example: When the new executive arrived at the company, he asked a manager to prepare a report summarizing sales force production for the previous year. He said he wanted the report as soon as possible. The manager had the needed information at hand, so he organized it and prepared a report, then submitted it the same day.

Two days later, the executive called the manager into his office and said, "You put a lot of pressure on me by giving me the report so soon after I asked for it. I felt compelled to respond in kind and for the last two days I've been worried about it." The manager was perplexed by this criticism and asked, "Well, was the report what you wanted?" The executive said, "I haven't had a chance to look at it yet."

This is typical of the problems you face when you take assignments seriously. Being early and even making deadlines can become big negatives. Some suggestions for dealing with this problem (see Figure 10-3):

1. *Don't change your style.* If you are able to produce excellent work quickly, don't let other people's insecurities make you change your work habits. Fast, accurate work *is* a positive attribute.

2. *Hold off until the deadline.* Making deadlines—even though it should be required—is exceptional enough, and a number of assignments come in late or not at all. So always meet deadlines when you promise to do so, but don't necessarily turn in work early. Complete assignments but, if you're early, hold off until the deadline.

Figure 10-3. Guidelines: fast response.

1. Don't change your style.

2. Hold off until the deadline.

3. Question criticism.

4. Make fast response a positive trait.

5. Ensure high quality.

3. *Question criticism.* Whenever people complain to you about your work coming in too fast, ask why it's a problem. If they are questioning the thoroughness or accuracy of a report, demand specifics. And if you find that it was prepared in haste, admit your error and take greater care the next time. But when a complaint has no real merit, state your opinion honestly. Question the criticism, and ask for clarification of the other people's thinking.

4. *Make fast response a positive trait.* Don't accept the premise that responding quickly is a negative trait. When people need answers quickly, they will come to you first. This is a valuable reputation to build. Even those who tend to criticize fast work will invariably turn to you when they're in a bind.

5. *Ensure high quality.* Those who ask for fast turnaround might not truly expect it. But when they get a good response, they often are suspicious and might look for errors rather than checking to see whether the assignment was completed correctly. With this in mind, you must impose a standard on yourself for exceptionally high quality. Once you develop the reputation for fast *and* accurate work, you will gain the respect that professional response deserves.

THE POSTMEETING

Meetings are often complicated by the nature of agenda topics and related assignments, to the extent that you might need a smaller meeting afterward. Your purpose may be to clarify an assignment, to ask for help from someone else, or to better define the approach you will take in solving the problem.

Organize postmeetings along the same guidelines you use as an attendee. Always define your purpose and goals, explain the problem to the other person or persons in attendance, and ask for their help. Be sure to conclude with answers. Invite those people who can help you to clear up or expand on what was discussed during the larger meeting.

Most postmeetings will involve one other person. Chances are, you will need additional information or assistance from a department head, your supervisor, or the meeting leader. If you find that one meeting necessitates another that's just as involved, you must review how well you have been able to establish your priorities during the original meeting.

It's quite likely that the problems you run into after the meeting are connected directly to the format or to the approach you took in preparation. You can eliminate most of those problems—and the need for extensive postmeetings—by fine-tuning your preparation technique and by doing everything you can to improve the tone and emphasis of the meetings you attend.

As a responsible manager, you have the duty to point out flaws in procedures your company practices. This includes meetings. It is politically sensitive to criticize any individual, so your comments must be directed at the process that is flawed, not at the people in charge of it. Criticism can always be expressed in positive terms that do not offend or threaten others. Much misunderstanding develops, though, because someone doesn't take the time to plan out criticisms with other people's sensitivities in mind.

POSTMEETING ACTION CHECKLIST

Follow these guidelines for your actions after meetings:

1. *Be sure you are given a specific assignment before proceeding.* If you need clarification, visit with the meeting leader or your supervisor and make sure you're expected to proceed.

2. *Involve others in the completion of your assignment.* The team approach will work outside of the meeting, just as it works during the meeting itself.

3. *When you meet with resistance from someone else, confront the resistance and not the person.* Find out *why* the other person will not help, and make every effort to explain your goals.

4. *Document your request.* Send other people a memo explaining your project, its purpose, and the way that you want their help.

5. *Use the chain of command.* If you should go through someone's supervisor to make a request, don't try to bypass the protocol.

6. *Be aware of time and resource constraints for the other people.* Their resistance might not be directed at you. They might simply not have the time nor the people available to respond as quickly as you'd like.

7. *Once you do get others to agree to your request, follow up with a clarifying memo.* List the points of agreement and conclusion. If the other people perceived your meeting differently, your memo gives them the chance to contact you and clear the air.

8. *Always acknowledge other people's help.* You can expect cooperation in the future when you show your gratitude. Also, let the other people's supervisor know that you appreciate their help and that the people came through in a professional manner.

9. *Never miss a deadline.* Set a standard for yourself that, as a meeting participant, you will always submit promised work by the deadline, without fail.

10. *If you complete work early, you should submit it only after checking for accuracy.* If early completion creates a problem for other people, consider holding the results until the deadline.

WORK PROJECT

1. List three strategies for dealing with a bureaucracy, and explain how they improve your ability to complete assignments after the meeting.

2. Describe three sensible rules for asking for help from outside of your department, and state how these points will improve chances for getting help.

3. List two guidelines for fast response to assignments, and explain how they help build your reputation in the company.

11

Politics for Attendees

It were not best that we should all think alike; it is difference of opinion that makes horseraces.

—Mark Twain

"I wasn't invited to the last two weekly meetings," Linda told her friend Kathy. "What does that mean?"
   Kathy answered: "You always say those meetings are a waste of time. So what's the problem?"
   "Having to go was bad enough," Linda said. "But not being asked . . . that really hurts."

The environment of the meeting represents opportunities waiting to be taken by you. Nowhere else in the company is there so much going on that remains unspoken, and nowhere else is corporate life as complicated. Still, by recognizing the opportunities to take positive action, you can make the meeting a constructive and worthwhile part of your professional experience.
   We must recognize the political aspects of meetings and learn to deal with them in positive ways. We all contend with political issues, and they do not have to be negatives. Being able to posture yourself to create a productive meeting environment is not enough. Every corporate manager must also be able to make the most of the public meeting forum.

We refer to meetings as "public" in the corporate sense, because they are the place where individuals voice their ideas, complain, request, argue, and decide. In every meeting, coalitions or individuals struggle to attain or increase their relative power and influence in the company. Power and influence, when used to create action and results, are not negatives any more than other political realities; it all depends on how they are used.

THE NEED FOR DISAGREEMENT

Even if you have attended only a few meetings, you already know that the agenda does not always list the real purpose. Meetings might be useful sessions for resolving and discussing issues and then deciding on a plan of action, serving as productive work sessions. But that's the case only if you and other attendees create a productive forum. Within the context of achieving a decision—which is a basic requirement for the successful meeting—you must be able to perceive what's really going on in the meeting.

It's rare that a meeting is called simply to discuss a problem, decide on a course of action, and make assignments to the appropriate departments. The individual who calls a meeting will perceive its purpose in a different manner than you and your fellow attendees. The written agenda is only the visible segment of what might be a much larger agenda, from many points of view.

It is virtually impossible to approach a question that is raised during a meeting with a clear, fully objective point of view. We all ask ourselves, "How does this affect me?" and a How does this affect my department?"

When you multiply this reality by the number of people at the meeting, it becomes evident that each person at the meeting will apply these questions; each one has a responsibility to take that approach. We must take care of our personal and career interests, and the interests of our department. No problem raised during a meeting can be approached without an individual perspective. When you attend a meeting, evaluate what's going on from your point of view, as well as from the point of view that is held by others.

Example: A marketing manager discusses the problems of monitoring production. He is concerned with developing a workable system for ensuring that the standard set for the department will be met. However, others in the same meeting have a different point of view. The accountant might resist any changes because they mean more work. The data processing manager resists having to alter programs and create a revised data base. And the vice-president of finance does not want to hear about new systems; he wants to know why sales figures for the last quarter are below forecast.

Each person has a different perspective on the problem and a different understanding of what solution is required. Motives, desired end results, and even the simple agreement about what is wrong, will inhibit the group from easily reaching a meaningful conclusion during a meeting.

In realizing that meetings do not always reach a decision point quickly, remember these guidelines (see Figure 11-1):

1. *Accept discussion as a requirement.* Before any agreement can be reached, a period of discussion is both necessary and productive. This

Figure 11-1. Debate guidelines.

1. Accept discussion as a requirement.

2. Point out differences of opinion.

3. Raise opposing points of view.

4. Begin arguments with a premise.

5. Recognize motives.

applies not only to debating solutions to a generally understood problem; it might be necessary just to define the problem itself.

2. *Point out differences of opinion.* Look for opportunities to point out differences of opinion. It could be that a lengthy discussion is an exercise in communication, or it could go nowhere—because two sides have a completely dissimilar view of the problem itself. You can contribute a lot by voicing the obvious differences.

3. *Raise opposing points of view.* As a participant, you will not be harmed by raising different ideas. In fact, when you are attempting to make a point, it will strengthen your position to address the same issue from another's perspective. During the period of discussion, debate is a positive and constructive exercise—as long as the attendees are in agreement about what problem is being aired.

4. *Begin arguments with a premise.* A constructive debate can take place only if everyone involved is on the same track. You will achieve much more by ensuring this than you will by simply giving your opinions.

Example: You begin your argument with the statement, "As I see it, the problem is. . . ." This opening is likely to result in more constructive response than your strongest argument, because it will bring to the surface any assumptions that conflict with yours. And that's a very positive result.

5. *Recognize motives.* It may be politically misguided to speak inappropriately during a meeting, even when addressing an issue directly. You must be aware of what drives other attendees and the meeting leader. By recognizing the points of view held by others at the meeting, you will be able to avoid offending your fellow attendees. Stick to the issues, but also seek definition.

Example: One participant argues against a proposed change in procedures. Even though everyone knows that the old procedures are not working, one manager is strongly opposed. You recognize that the suggested change would mean his department will have to drastically change the way it operates. You can help clear the air by vocalizing the problem and by pointing out that the solution has ramifications that must be discussed and resolved.

The unspoken nature of many problems at work during a meeting makes meaningful communication difficult. You will achieve the most by vocalizing the political realities that pervade the meeting and by attempting to give equal weight to different points of view. And no matter how pure your motives, you will find it impossible to achieve any real progress in meetings without understanding their political side.

DEALING WITH THE SELF-SERVING POSTURE

Doing all you can to ensure a productive meeting is one positive way to make internal politics work. It is much more difficult to deal with the situation in which someone else uses a meeting to serve his or her own purposes.

We generally assume that agenda items are included for a general discussion and, hopefully, resolution. Some meetings, though, are used by individuals to exert their power and influence at the expense of others.

Example: A vice-president was in the habit of gathering managers together for meetings once or twice per week. Whenever someone voiced a dissenting opinion to a position the vice-president held, he reacted very poorly and defensively.

Public confrontations such as that are very difficult to witness and counterproductive to the meeting's purpose. How can you deal with this situation? Some suggested guidelines (see Figure 11-2):

1. *Be aware of the meeting's purpose.* When a meeting turns into a personality conflict, you have very little power to directly alter the situation. However, you can protect yourself from political consequences. Be aware of the way that some people lead meetings and accept the inevitable: You'll never have the chance to participate in some types of meetings unless you are willing to take great risks.

2. *Achieve results outside of the meeting.* You cannot depend on the meeting for the constructive results you desire, so you must find other ways to achieve. If possible, do not attend "limelight" meetings, since

Figure 11-2. Guidelines for dealing with negative meetings.

1. Be aware of the meeting's purpose.

2. Achieve results outside of the meeting.

3. Do not become involved.

4. Maintain a neutral position.

5. Complain only through channels.

they are a waste of time. But if you must attend, don't add to the meeting's length by offering any opinions or ideas.

3. *Do not become involved.* Stay out of the line of fire when two or more people become involved in a disagreement at a poorly led meeting. Recognize that there's little you can do to change a negative situation. The best response is to keep your distance and to seek more positive environments in which to express yourself.

4. *Maintain a neutral position.* Don't let yourself be forced into one camp or another. Internal power struggles involve a great deal of wasted time and energy, with each side trying to line up allies. Stay out of the fight, and concentrate on the tasks you're supposed to accomplish.

5. *Complain only through channels.* If you believe you must complain about a negative situation, go through the proper channels. Start with your direct supervisor and ask that your message be passed along to the next level.

THE ASSERTIVE RESPONSE

You might want to speak out concerning meetings that are not working. Doing so means you must take a risk, and an evaluation of your company's top management must determine the likely response. Will you place your career in jeopardy by asserting yourself? Top managers invariably claim to encourage free-thinking and outspoken team members. In reality, some top managers do *not* want their people to question the system. You will have to decide for yourself whether they are sincere in encouraging you to take a stand—even the *right* stand.

This reality serves as a general guideline that everyone may follow, both in meetings and in every other forum for interaction. If the meeting is being misused in any way, you have the right to point it out. But before you do, assess the risk. Confronting a *problem* and not an abusive person is always right. Many of us are prevented from taking a stand, however, from fear of the possible cost.

Short of directly confronting a problem, you can assert yourself strongly by refusing to go along with the majority—just because popular opinion is also safe opinion. If you are willing to risk being known as a person who has a free mind and who speaks it, you will keep the more devious fellow employee off guard.

DIPLOMACY IN MEETINGS

The world's greatest diplomats do not reside in embassy buildings across the sea. They are found in boardrooms and conference rooms of every company. The real test of diplomacy is not in headlines, but in day-to-day survival without compromising principles.

Good diplomacy does not require patronizing a difficult person, nor compromising with a wrong point of view. More than anything else, it requires conviction and strength. A true diplomat, in those instances when right and wrong are clear, is able to stand up and speak the truth.

In every company, however, even the best top management must tolerate internal politics and, hopefully, use those politics as positive forces. Every employee must be able to time confrontations, or in some cases decide not to confront at all. Somewhere between absolute honesty and total deception, there is a middle ground. And that's where the diplomatic employee becomes a career survivor.

Apply these standards for maintaining a balance between speaking the truth and applying diplomacy (see Figure 11-3):

1. *Think before you speak.* The plain truth does not always work during a meeting. Just as you resent a confrontation in public, you cannot always question someone's statement publicly and expect a positive response. There is never only one way to convey an idea. Look for ways to dissent without challenging someone directly.

Figure 11-3. Balancing truth with diplomacy.

1. Think before you speak.

2. Phrase your arguments carefully.

3. Avoid speaking in absolutes.

4. Present fact over opinion.

5. Show respect for common beliefs.

6. Don't disagree just to make a point.

7. Keep an open mind.

2. *Phrase your arguments carefully.* Remember to confront only the issues at hand. Rather than disagreeing straight out, there may be ways to agree, with qualifications.

Example: During a budget meeting, the vice-president states that it is impossible to put a process to practical use. You strongly disagree. You can create an argument by offering a direct challenge. Or you can diplomatically offer, "I agree with your contention, given the lack of follow-up we've seen in the past. But what if we change the monthly review procedures?"

3. *Avoid speaking in absolutes.* You leave no room for discussion if you state that someone else is wrong and that's all there is to it. All that's left then is space for polarization and strengthening of opposite view-points. You will be more likely to win arguments if you can establish one point—even a small one—on which you and the other person agree, and proceed from there.

4. *Present fact over opinion.* When you present a dissenting idea, you are always assumed to have only an opinion. The majority might doubt and resist you. Therefore, you must be prepared to defend your opinion with hard, indisputable facts. An opinion is always weak if it's perceived to be wrong or even unpopular. But facts speak for themselves.

5. *Show respect for common beliefs.* Many popular and common beliefs are weak when examined logically and even when merely questioned. But you cannot win your point by ridiculing the beliefs or by stating that they are foolish. Either work around the common misconceptions, or make your points in the context of those beliefs.

6. *Don't disagree just to make a point.* You can harm your reputation if you disagree too often during meetings. As a rule, you will not find the opportunity to present yourself as a free-thinking individual in every meeting. Becoming known as someone who questions everything will result in a loss of respect, and you will hold less influence in the long run. The day will come when taking a strong stand is appropriate; wait patiently for that time, rather than looking for chances to set yourself apart.

7. *Keep an open mind.* If you are willing to state an unpopular opinion, you must also be ready to change your mind. In some cases the

majority is right, perhaps for reasons that are not evident to you. Once you see a new dimension to the issue, be willing to admit your error and back down.

MAKING POLITICS A PLUS

Attendees who want to attend productive, worthwhile meetings might find themselves at a disadvantage. The meeting leader should be in control; however, when that control is not applied, you will want to assert yourself without creating the appearance of trying to control the meeting.

This is a sensitive and difficult problem. The only workable solution is to persist in asking for definition. Even the poorest meeting leader will not be able to deny the validity of your insistent but diplomatic request.

Shrewd meeting etiquette requires that any vocal forays you take must be made with respect for the leader, even when true leadership is not being exercised. The problem you face in nudging a meeting along its rightful course may be exhausting and risky; but when the course is not being followed, the meeting is not proceeding along the best path, one that leads to positive actions.

You can make the undercurrents of political activity in meetings a plus. By respecting the leader's role, you can make your point strongly without offending the leader.

There is no fault in prefacing your comments with statements demonstrating your awareness of the leader. For example, you might use one of these statements:

- "This is your meeting—I don't want to presume. However . . ."
- "As I understand your purpose . . ."
- "Do you agree with the premise that . . ."

A strong leader will be grateful for the gentle reminder, while a week leader will not view your statement as a challenge. And if you do inadvertently offend the leader by any statement you make, meet with him or her immediately after the meeting, and apologize. By keeping open an honest and sincere line of communication—especially with those who become angry with you—the political realities in your organization can be turned from a negative to a positive factor.

WORK PROJECT

1. A meeting you attend ends up as a debate among several managers. Name two guidelines you should use to participate in this type of meeting.

2. List two guidelines for action during a meeting that has a negative tone, and explain how these ideas will help you deal with the politics in your company.

3. Explain two points worth remembering on how to balance truth with diplomacy during meetings.

12

Creating the
Best Environment

Be a leader in meetings. Even those you don't chair.

—Thomas L. Quick

"To make your meetings work, you'll have to offer a more comprehensive agenda," the experienced manager told his young colleague after a first attempt at leading. "Your attendees will respond to only two things. First is a discussion of topics that interest and concern them."
"What's the second thing?"
"A catered lunch."

Meetings provide you with the chance to actively contribute to solutions and to create profits in your organization, whether you participate as a leader or an attendee. As a forum for the expression of ideas, meetings will demonstrate your value to management. But that can be achieved only if you are able to solve problems, work around the bureaucracy, and keep the organization's priorities in mind.

As a meeting leader, you are not only in a position to execute agenda problems in terms of action and follow-up; you are also in a position to motivate others. And as a well-motivated attendee, you can become a meeting leader's most valuable ally and resource. When that occurs, you not only improve the meeting environment; you also improve the way that you are perceived as a resource in the organization.

MAXIMIZING THE LEADERSHIP ROLE

You can act in a leadership capacity even when you are not the meeting leader. In one respect, leadership is demonstrated by being willing to volunteer for assignments or even to help others with their assigned projects.

The attempt to create a positive, results–oriented meeting is the responsibility of all attendees—not just the designated meeting leader. As a leader, you will improve by remaining flexible and structuring your role to the circumstances at hand. Constant evaluation of your own performance will improve that role and will enable you to overcome problems experienced in past meetings.

Leaders can improve their performance in preparation and planning, running the meeting, and follow–up, by taking these steps:

1. *Evaluate past meetings.* Look for areas in which you would like to improve, and concentrate on developing those skills.
2. *Invite critical evaluation and suggestions from your attendees.* Listen carefully. And then make every effort to improve, based on the advice you hear.
3. *When reaction to your efforts at follow-up are negative, analyze the reasons.* Was your approach overly aggressive? Was your attitude unintentionally offensive? What pressures was the other person under, which you failed to recognize?
4. *Speak to other meeting leaders, especially those whose meetings you have attended.* What areas can you improve? How have they overcome the same difficulties?
5. *Never settle for just one formula for meeting success.* Even when one approach works for a particular meeting, you must remain flexible. Different meeting formats place different demands on

leaders, and the best way to manage an agenda and a group will vary from one situation to another.

Every attendee can benefit the meeting through enthusiastic and properly directed motivation. Think of meetings as opportunities to do your best work, to gain endorsement for your efforts, and to test ideas by exposing them to constructive group criticism and examination.

Attendees can improve their level of participation and value as members of the group, with these ideas:

1. *Speak to meeting leaders.* Find out what they want and expect from you. Ask, "How can I make myself valuable to you as an attendee?"
2. *Evaluate the leaders' ability to motivate attendees.* Look for their strong points as well as their flaws. Alter your level of participation so that the meeting can be its most productive.
3. *Discuss recurring meetings with others who attend.* Find out what perceptions they hold, and compare those to your own. You might identify common elements that are flawed, and you can then work together to improve the meeting's quality in the future.
4. *Never settle for a passive role during a meeting.* Seek ways to make a contribution, even when someone else is given primary responsibility for a task.

You must be aware of a leader's sensitivity to any ideas you propose. That individual might have a possessive attitude about "her" meetings. So you have to approach the problem with the leader's consent and full agreement. To achieve this, follow these guidelines (see Figure 12-1):

1. *Define the problem in positive terms.* Whenever a problem is defined as a negative, the ensuing debate probably will prevent a constructive dialogue. Instead, a group debates the problem and presents opposing negative points of view. But when a problem is expressed in a positive way, the path is cleared for definition and agreement.

Example: During a staff meeting, you want to raise the issue of poor communication. You're aware that several other managers *avoid* working together; however, you do not raise that as the issue. Instead,

Figure 12-1. Guidelines: solving the leadership problem.

1. Define the problem in positive terms.

2. Remove the personality issue.

3. Accept responsibility.

4. Seek solutions by asking questions.

5. Involve the meeting leader.

you identify specific ideas to improve communication in a way that you believe is nonthreatening.

2. *Remove the personality issue.* You might complain, "That guy doesn't know how to lead a meeting." This only focuses on the individual assumed to be in control, and his or her failings. But if you avoid personalities, the issue becomes much clearer: "We need to resolve problems and reach decisions, and then act. The way we're operating now, that's not happening."

Example: The leader of a weekly meeting you attend is not effective in his job. You and other attendees share several problems that demand resolution. During the meeting, you raise an issue and also propose ideas for solutions. You tactfully assume the leadership role, knowing that the designated leader will not take that step.

3. *Accept responsibility.* If you throw up your hands and refuse to take part in solving a group's problems, then the problems can never be solved. Take responsibility as a member of the group, and don't just assume that it's up to the leader to do all of the work.

Example: You have been frustrated at having to attend lengthy meetings where nothing seems to get done. But rather than allowing yourself to become apathetic about the entire process, you start asking for definition whenever an agenda item is being discussed. The result: Decisions are made and assignments given out.

4. *Seek solutions by asking questions.* Rather than trying to make a statement about the meeting problem, ask the group to define the solution for you. This technique can be used even during the meeting itself, in front of the ineffective leader, without offending anyone. You can ask the leader to conclude discussions, suggesting that a solution must be developed, actions decided, and assignments given out. If this is done with discretion, the passive leader probably will not notice that you're performing the leadership role.

Example: During a long discussion about a problem, you see that nothing conclusive is happening. You speak up and ask, "Now that we've explored the problem, what solutions should we come up with?"

5. *Involve the meeting leader.* Your best ally in resolving the problem is the meeting leader (who is perceived in many cases as the *source* or even as the problem itself). Approach the leader and ask that your idea be placed on the next agenda.

Example: You approach a meeting leader and present your plan. You explain, "These problems are especially complex, and we've been having trouble getting to resolution of the agenda. Here's an idea that will help us to overcome the problem and at the same time make your job easier."

Here's a way that these guidelines can be applied to resolve the problem of unfocused, unproductive meetings (the guidelines are in italic):

You approach the leader of an upcoming monthly managers' meeting *(involve the meeting leader)* and state that you have developed an idea for creating decisions and action *(accept responsibility)*. You ask the leader to put this on the agenda *(remove the personality issue)*. You comment that it will solve the problem of making decisions as a group, which is always difficult *(define the problem in positive terms)*. During the meeting you begin the discussion by asking, "What's the best way to decide what we must do to solve the problems we talk about in this meeting?" *(seek solutions by asking questions)*

You can lead the group to the logical conclusion that the important, action-oriented questions should be asked to resolve each agenda item: What is the problem, how can I help, who is responsible, and what action should be taken? When you express the problem as a question, the group will be more likely to become involved. Rather than being told to passively accept *your* definition of a problem, everyone—including the leader—has the chance to participate in coming up with a constructive solution.

WORKING WITH THE COMMITTEE

Every business strives to maintain a balance between two extreme situations. In one, a single, autocratic leader runs the company, makes all decisions, and prevents anyone else from offering ideas, taking part in creating solutions, or even being made aware of priorities. In the other, a highly participative culture exists, in which management tries to make everyone feel completely involved—to the extent that nothing can get done because no one is in the position to make a decision.

The meeting should be designed to keep interaction in the company in between the extremes—with a healthy degree of contribution from employees, but without the bureaucracy that strangles corporate action.

As a company grows in size—in terms of geography, volume, and employees—the tendency toward the more bureaucratic state is a dangerous trend worth avoiding. A growing organization faces the threat that a once effective team will decline to an ineffective string of committees, with no one able to act or even willing to recognize that a problem exists.

You probably can do little to change an existing bureaucracy, but you can do a lot to ensure that your meetings are as effective as possible. The bureaucracy does not come into being for devious reasons; most often, it is the consequence of well-intended actions for documentation and tracking that have simply gone too far.

Example: Your department is invited to weekly staff meetings that never result in positive action or decisions. In your opinion these meetings are not productive. You have tried to change the situation by asking the right questions, but that hasn't worked.

The solution: Identify the problems of concern to your department, and develop ideas for solutions. When those ideas involve other departments, hold limited meetings and propose action. Reduce your participation in the larger, less effective meeting, to reporting on your independent decisions and actions.

Several potential problems can arise from this approach, and they must be addressed:

1. *Creation of a larger bureaucracy.* By putting together your own system of meetings, you could create a larger problem. Many individuals in business and government have tried to reduce the bureaucracy by creating new committees or departments. You must ensure that your independent meeting simplifies, leads to action, and does not grow on its own.

2. *Power threats.* Executives and other managers might see your outside actions as an attempt to build your own "empire." You could become a perceived threat to the existing power. Remember that people resist change, that they are aware of relative power and influence, and that they do not always understand your motives. The solution is to let results speak for you and to use power and influence appropriately and sparingly. Don't get tied up in the struggle for perception of power; concentrate on making sure your meetings are efficient, short, and productive.

3. *Approval.* A manager should have the right to call meetings to resolve problems for a department or section. But when you invite attendees from other departments, you could create a problem for your supervisor. If you need approval before you proceed, be sure that you explain your reasons well and that your supervisor endorses your plan.

EVALUATING YOUR MEETINGS

Evaluation is the key to improvement. Only by judging your participation and leadership in a meeting setting can you expect to improve performance in the future.

After concluding a meeting, answer these questions:

1. Did you confront the issues?

Leaders: Did you lead the group through the agenda, take a stand on tough issues, and seek definition of the solution? Did you bring the meeting to the point of decision? Were assignments made?

Attendees: Did you speak out and state your position when the opportunity presented itself? Were you able to support your position with facts? How can you improve your posture in future meetings?

2. Did you perform the way you wanted to?

Leaders: Were you firm and assertive and, at the same time, fair to all attendees? Did you encourage others to speak out and state their ideas?

Attendees: Did you help the leader in achieving the meeting's purpose? How could you make yourself more useful as an active participant?

3. How did you handle new ideas?

Leaders: Were new ideas raised? If so, were you open-minded to the possibilities? Did you give the speaker a fair opportunity to explain?

Attendees: Did you look at the issues with a fresh approach? If you had any new ideas, did you verbalize them? How will you deal with these questions in future meetings?

4. Did you practice participation?

Leaders: Were you fair in the way you handled the group? Did you make certain that everyone had the chance to speak out? Did you ask questions and delegate well?

Attendees: Did you look for ways to make your attendance count? Did you volunteer for assignments? How can you improve your value in future meetings?

5. Did you act to improve meeting quality?

Leaders: Did you take any specific actions to make your meeting better than the one before? Can you identify steps to take now that will make the next meeting better?

Attendees: How could you alter your participation to add even more value to the meeting? Have you spoken to the leader and offered to help? Have you studied the agenda for your next meeting?

MEETINGS AND YOUR CAREER

On the premise that your company's management grants you the freedom to act, you can create the types of meetings that are productive and get results. At the same time, meetings can become the forum for advancing in your career—in an extremely positive way.

Every action you take within the organization creates response. As long as you are aware of how your statements and actions affect others, you can become an influential participant in creating the positive mood that all people prefer in their working life. This ideal might fail when individuals forget how to communicate with one another and allow themselves to become part of a committee mentality. Attending or leading a meeting is a most rewarding experience when a team functions well—not as a bureaucracy that inhibits decisions, but as a group of people with a singular purpose.

There is no conflict between the human need for recognition as individuals and the more remote corporate desire for profits. In fact, the more successful companies pay closer attention to the needs of employees than do the organizations that never achieve a competitive leadership role. All employees want to feel included and know that their contribution counts. But merely allowing someone to attend a meeting does not address that desire. Real participation—which also means being able to improve a meeting that isn't working—is more difficult to achieve in a large organization.

An examination of successful companies invariably reveals a satisfied, productive, and outspoken management team. When a company's leadership encourages employees to think and express their thoughts, continuing progress is not only possible—it's inevitable. A company led from the top with the support and enthusiasm of its employees is destined to succeed. The satisfied, involved employee of a progressive organization is able to speak out, not only in one-to-one communications, but in meetings as well.

You can test the quality of your company by examining the types of meetings it allows. An increasing number of meetings, especially those between company executives, is rarely a sign of improved communication, contrary to what some people believe. It doesn't matter how many meetings take place, but what—if anything—happens as the result of bringing people together.

You prove your worth to the organization when you participate in a productive way, either as an attendee or a leader. When you attend meetings, ask the right questions and accept responsibilities; then come through by the deadline. If specific assignments, responsibilities, and deadlines are not given out, insist on that minimal level of decision. And whenever a discussion takes place without defining a precise problem, ask for a clear consensus and agreement—or at least start the debate that will begin to define the problem.

As a meeting leader, you have the opportunity to show your abilities to get others to act. You must play several roles: careful organizer, accomplished diplomat, and deft time manager. You must delegate with authority and fairness, deal with the disruptive attendee, and encourage the introvert to speak out. You must be able to assert control, even when someone who outranks you tries to take over your meeting—without making an enemy or creating a confrontation.

The techniques for balancing all of these concerns are not difficult to master. But they are mandatory if you want to have the reputation as one who is able to lead. The meeting is a place to demonstrate your abilities, in a more public way than in any other form of communication in the organization. Thus, the meeting is not just a waste of time that you have no power to change; it is the opportunity to build a career, by showing that you are a valuable participant and leader.

The real leadership does not always come from the designated meeting leader. Even if you are only one of many attendees, you can demonstrate your leadership ability. Your understanding of a problem, or even your ability to clearly ask for definition, might prove to be the most important quality of leadership in the meeting. And when you accept responsibility and come through with results, you will be perceived as the most essential manager, the kind that every executive wants to work with.

WORK PROJECT

1. List two ideas that will solve the problem of poor leadership. How will these ideas improve meetings?

2. List the potential problems in working outside of the existing bureaucracy, and explain how those problems must be solved.

Appendix
Work Project Answers

CHAPTER 1

1. Meetings without agendas cannot possibly be organized, for a number of reasons. First, every attendee—if expected to participate—must be given time to prepare. Second, each person invited to the meeting must be given the chance to suggest agenda items. Third, an agenda is necessary in order to manage the time that the meeting will require.

   Time limits must be set and enforced. The greater the number of attendees, the more critical the time factor becomes. A well-planned meeting will always include a definition of starting and ending time.

   Suggest the following:
   a. An agenda should be prepared well in advance of the meeting and sent to all people invited to attend. They should also have the chance to comment and make suggestions about agenda items.
   b. Recommend that starting time should be announced and enforced, and that the meeting should end at a predesignated time. This will help keep the meeting on track.
   c. Suggest that each attendee participate in some way, either by presenting the topic of an agenda item or by being asked to comment and offer solutions.
2. The myths concerning meetings include
   a. The number of attendees defines a quality team. Reality: Smaller groups are more efficient. Make this point to reduce attendance at meetings that do not work in your company.
   b. Frequent meetings improve communication. Reality: Real communication is the product of action. Make a change by suggesting to management that a smaller number of meetings with fewer participants will achieve more.
   c. Interaction leads to solutions. Reality: Solutions come from hard work. Interaction may play a role in arriving at alternatives, but

you also need an action plan. If none is proposed, raise it during the meetings you attend.

   d. Taking action is the leader's role. Reality: Attendees are responsible for follow-up action. The leader moderates the discussion and controls the agenda. Always raise the question of responsibility and follow-up, and force the group to make decisions.

   e. Meetings lead to consensus. Reality: People interpret meetings in different ways. Never assume that everyone has drawn the same conclusions after a meeting. To ensure that key decisions are in consensus, follow up after a meeting with a memo that restates actions and reinforces deadlines.

   f. Free expression defines a successful meeting. Reality: Discussion alone cannot lead to action. Always bring up the question of who will do what, and by what deadline.

3. The four questions are

   a. Who is responsible for solving this problem?

   b. How can the rest of us help?

   c. What course of action should be taken?

   d. What's the deadline?

By raising these questions for each agenda item and in every meeting you attend, you force others to address the issues required for real solutions. You will have a direct influence on improving the quality of meetings in your company.

CHAPTER 2

1. Meetings should be called for the following reasons:

   a. Problems are common to the group. They will be best resolved with an open discussion, while you cannot expect any final agreement when the involved people never get together. The meeting, in this case, will prove far more effective than individual communication.

   b. Information is needed in both directions. A meeting is most valuable when everyone—including the leader—learns from the experience. Shared information helps everyone in attendance.

c. Decisions are to be made collectively. A meeting is the best forum for true teamwork. However, the teamwork idea is often distorted into a means for shifting responsibility or for achieving nothing at all. The meeting is an effective place for teamwork, as long as teamwork is really practiced.

d. Responsibility is not clear. Meetings can clear the air and bring out assumptions and conflicts. Individual meetings never resolve anything when individuals have conflicting points of view.

e. The group wants to meet with you. As long as there are valid, worthwhile reasons to get together, a meeting can be useful and productive. However, avoid the problem of creating a permanent meeting when there is no recurring need for an agenda.

2. You do not need to call a meeting when:

a. Issues require singular communication. If a problem can be resolved by meeting with one other person, there's no reason to call a group together.

b. You don't have a specific agenda. Never call a general-purpose meeting. Without problems to resolve and specific goals, the meeting will not achieve any results.

c. Issues should be discussed privately. Don't use the meeting as a place to confront others or to discuss personnel policies or salary increases.

d. Another form of communication is better. A letter, memo, or telephone call might be a better way to get results; in those cases, you do not need a meeting.

e. A decision has already been made. Don't raise a question if you already know the answer. That will only create negative response and, if others disagree with you, an argument.

3. The agenda should include:

a. title: give each meeting a name, so that others can identify it without confusion.

b. time and location: include starting and ending time, date, and place.

c. theme and definition: briefly describe the scope and purpose of your meeting.

d. attendees: list names and titles of those who will attend, and indicate which person will lead the meeting.

e. topics: for each agenda item, include a title, brief description, and your goal for the meeting.

CHAPTER 3

1. Identify the proper people to invite with these guidelines:
   a. problem-solving meetings:
      Who should be on hand to solve problems?
      Who has a direct interest in the solution?
   b. status meetings:
      Who is directly involved and responsible?
      Who can influence progress of the job?
   c. information meetings:
      Who needs to know?
      Who has information you need?
   d. work meetings:
      Who will actually do the work?
2. When someone asks for a separate meeting, ask:
   a. What do you need to discuss? In many cases, the topic will be brief enough to have a one- or two-minute meeting on the spot.
   b. Why can't we cover it at the regular meeting? Avoid duplicating effort by covering the same material twice; the topic might belong in the larger group.
   c. Who else should be in on the discussion? This might reveal that, in fact, the subject should be covered in front of everyone.

CHAPTER 4

1. Establishing strict rules and enforcing them is essential to effective leadership. Include these points in your rules:
   a. The agenda is preannounced: It's essential that attendees be given time to prepare for your agenda. Never hold a meeting when you have not been given at least one day to tell your participants what your meeting will involve.

b. Attendance is verified: You must be able to find out, in advance, whether invited people will come to your meeting. If they are essential to your agenda, a no-show will require altering your agenda.

c. Meetings will not be interrupted: Don't allow employees to enter the meeting room with questions or messages after you've started, and don't let meeting attendees receive phone calls during the meeting.

d. The agenda will be followed: Be sure you cover all of the topics on your agenda, and don't allow other subjects to be introduced.

e. A specific result will be achieved: Set the goal that your meetings will always have a purpose—to solve a problem, identify the need for action, or make assignments. Then be sure to achieve the meeting's goal before you adjourn.

f. The meeting leader is identified: You have the right to expect everyone in attendance to respect your authority as a leader, even if some attendees outrank you. Insist on being given authority to accompany the responsibility you have as meeting leader.

2. Meeting rules should be summarized for attendees, with emphasis on the agenda and start and stop times. You should also propose a formal procedure and policy statement to management, with the recommendation that your guidelines be adopted for all internal meetings. If management will not endorse and approve your idea, proceed with rules for the meetings you lead. Let attendees know what you expect, and enforce the rules you set.

3. When attendees do not offer ideas, ask questions, or take part in discussions, ask yourself:

a. How can I encourage others to participate more in the meeting? Some employees will have excellent ideas, but fear speaking out. As a meeting leader, you can play an important part in helping them develop their self-confidence as meeting participants.

b. What topics are of specific interest to each member? Once you identify this, you can relegate leadership during discussion of that topic.

c. Do I enforce the rules so strictly that no one is willing to speak up? If you think you're exerting too strongly, it might be time to back off. Let a meeting take its natural course, and step in only if the discussion wanders away from the agenda.

CHAPTER 5

1. Very few people will take action on their own initiative, and even when assignments have been agreed on, many will not come through without prompting and follow-up:
   a. Lay the groundwork well before the meeting. When you let people know in advance what assignments they're likely to receive, your meeting will run more smoothly.
   b. Make specific assignments. During the meeting, you must ensure that the job has been defined well enough for someone to take action. Without this, your meetings will not be productive.
   c. Write it down and send it out. The memo, by itself, is not the best form of communication. But it does help bring out any misunderstandings that develop from your meetings.
   d. Send copies to the right executives. Let those in positions of responsibility know what commitments have been made by their subordinates. This will help ensure that people follow through.
   e. Follow up in person. See each attendee who accepted an assignment, as soon after your meeting as possible. Be sure that the deadline will not pose a problem, offer your help, and ask to be kept up-to-date.
   f. Ask for help. If you cannot get a response from someone, go to your supervisor or the person to whom your attendee reports. You have the right to have commitments kept. If they are not, use the chain of command to get action.
   g. Use the most dependable resources. When you have to work too hard just to get someone else to keep a promise, it's a poor use of your time. Find out which people are dependable, and invite them to your meetings.
2. Minutes not only record what takes place in your meeting; they also keep the record straight. These points should always be listed:
   a. date and time
   b. attendees
   c. agenda topics discussed
   d. definition of problems (this helps you to deal with misunderstandings assigned people might develop otherwise)

    e. alternatives presented (in defining how to solve a problem, a summary of discussions helps guide the assigned person toward the best possible solution)

    f. solutions agreed on (this gives the actual guidelines for proceeding; if someone deviates, you will be able to refer to your minutes)

    g. assignments made and accepted (all those who accept an assignment will clearly understand what's expected of them)

    h. deadlines (an assignment demands a specific deadline, and that should be documented)

    i. follow-up actions (the minutes must state what actions will be taken, both by the person with the assignment and by the leader; this sets the rules for achieving desired results)

3. To delegate assignments, follow these rules:

    a. Identify responsibility. If you know who should do the job, state your position. When someone else disagrees, discussion can lead to an acceptable delegation of responsibility.

    b. Don't turn delegation around. Never let attendees give a job back to you, so that you end up doing all of the work yourself.

    c. Ask attendees who should do the job. The delegation process is made easier when you adopt a passive stance. Let the right people name themselves, and then ask for a deadline.

    d. Don't overload any one person. When an attendee accepts any and all assignments, that's a danger signal. As the leader, watch out for those who don't know their own work commitment limits.

    e. Beware of the silent attendee. If one of the people at your meeting never accepts an assignment, why did you invite her? Either she should be doing more, or you should drop her name from your list.

    f. Acknowledge a job well done. As a leader, show your appreciation to those who do come through with assignments.

CHAPTER 6

1. Quality circles are formal, structured meetings that enable employees to participate directly in solving common problems. Many of the

attributes of this form of meeting can be used to improve the meetings you hold. For example:

a. common interest: All those who attend your meetings must have common interests on the appropriate level. Otherwise, they will be unable to agree on definition of problems or on the correct solution.

b. voluntary basis: Everyone attending a quality circle meeting is there by choice. You cannot always set the same standard for the corporate meetings you lead, but it helps to have willing participants.

c. specific, defined projects: Quality circles are based on the absolute need for definition and consensus of problems to be addressed. In your meetings you do not have the freedom to pick and choose your own problems, but you must strive for clear definition and agreement about what the problem is.

d. clear leadership: A quality circle works only when one person is appointed as leader—regardless of corporate rank. This should be true of your meetings, although you will have more difficulty obtaining expressed, verbal agreement with this idea.

CHAPTER 7

1. Keep these points and examples in mind:

a. Keep the focus narrow: If you allow the discussions to wander away from the immediate issue, you will not be able to achieve the objectives of your meeting.

b. Use the argument of time: With constant awareness that a limited amount of time is available, you will be able to keep the meeting moving forward.

c. Keep follow-up notes: To ensure that your meetings result both in a decision and action, you must be able to monitor the progress made by attendees—either in future meetings or by direct supervision. Keeping notes of each meeting helps you to achieve this objective.

d. Don't add to the agenda: Consult with attendees in advance, and ask if they have any topics that should be included. But once the meeting begins, don't allow others to expand on the topics you plan to cover.

e. Stop on time: Even when you have not covered all of the topics on your agenda, stop your meetings on time. List the most critical problems first, and the lower priorities last, so that any missed items can be added to the agenda for the next meeting or can be resolved in meetings with fewer attendees.

2. The agenda provides these benefits:

a. organization: by putting down on paper the topics you plan to cover, and by arranging them in priority order, you ensure that the scope of the meeting is limited and defined.

b. preparation: an agenda helps attendees prepare in advance, so that they will be better able to participate.

c. time management: the agenda is an important tool for time management. It can be used as the reason for proceeding from one topic to another, for defining a narrow scope so that discussions will not become overly broad, or for helping others to provide answers through thorough preparation in advance of the meeting.

d. continuity: always carry unfinished business forward from one agenda to the next. Plan to check on the status of assignments and deadlines agreed on during past meetings, to ensure that attendees are coming through with what was promised.

CHAPTER 8

1. Proof in support of your ideas should be aimed at establishing improved profits or reduced costs and expenses. Corporate decisions ultimately are made on the basis of profit and loss. Proof may consist of analysis and estimation, or offering a better procedure.

Other points of view will arise, and the better prepared you are, the better able you will be to deal with conflict. Meet with other managers who will be affected by your ideas, before you make a presentation in a meeting setting. Deal with their point of view as you make your own case. By raising issues in the context of your best argument, you will reduce the disagreement considerably.

2. Guidelines include:
   a. Never present just one side. You are more likely to win your case when you present an idea that has already considered the problems and offers solutions to them.
   b. Always expect disagreement. A roomful of people who accept whatever you say without dissent is not a meeting at all. An active and capable group will challenge your ideas and force you to make your best case.
   c. Deal with conflict calmly. Always respond in defense of your issues, and refer to your proof as your best arguments.
   d. Confront issues and not people. Even when you believe an opposing point of view is critical of you personally, stay with the issues.
   e. Work around closed minds. The comments "We've never done it that way" and "It's not in the budget" are unimaginative but, in a sense, final points. You can get around these traditional arguments by asking, "If it wasn't for that, would you have a problem with the idea?"
3. There are several good reasons for a premeeting. Among these are:
   a. Your ideas may affect another department. As a matter of courtesy, you should let others know what you are planning to propose.
   b. Other managers may raise points you have not yet considered. By incorporating these into your idea, you add dimension while solving problems.
   c. Your ideas may be inappropriate for presentation at a particular meeting. An objective outsider might see this, where you could miss the point.

CHAPTER 9

1. Meetings are defined when you follow three guidelines:
   a. Define participation. You must know how you are expected to make a contribution, or else you cannot be of any value in the meeting. By insisting on this definition, you will be part of a working team; without it, you are only a member of the passive audience.

b. Be prepared to offer an opinion. Having opinions or good ideas is of no value unless you also have the right to voice them. If everyone with ideas insists on speaking out at meetings, that alone will force meetings to become more useful and worthwhile.

c. Use the chain of command. Make it an advantage rather than a handicap. You can delegate to executives as long as the solutions to problems rightly belong at the top.

2. No matter how complex a report or issue, it can be explained very briefly, in five steps:

a. Define the problem. A one- or two-sentence explanation clears the air and ensures that all attendees—speaker and listeners—are discussing the same problem.

b. Methods. Briefly explain how a problem has been approached, or how you suggest a solution should be arrived at. The right method will be dictated by the nature of the problem.

c. Information sources. Refer to written or historical information, or to resources inside or outside the organization, for development of solutions.

d. Conclusions. State precise, unqualified conclusions to the problem. A specific, strongly stated position conveys confidence and is a convincing way to win your point.

e. Recommendations. Suggest (or ask) who should be responsible for action, what precise actions should be taken, and what deadlines should be agreed on.

CHAPTER 10

1. Guidelines for dealing with a bureaucracy include:

a. Get a specific assignment. Clear definition is a practical defense to the bureaucratic way of thinking, and with it you can guide your actions with more focus.

b. Take the team approach. Ask others to work with you, rather than simply cooperating in your effort. Even when a team is not actually at work, others may respond better when they think in terms of a team effort.

    c. Confront resistance. If possible, discuss the problem you're having with the source. Or, if that isn't possible, go to your supervisor and ask for help.

    d. Write a memo. And be sure to send a copy to the other person's supervisor. This might prompt a response, and also protects you in the event you're not able to complete your assignment by the deadline.

    e. Submit an incomplete report. You can make your point by simply working around the source of resistance.

    f. Get your facts elsewhere. Neutralize the bureaucracy by letting it know you do not need it.

2. Whenever you deal with someone in another department, follow these guidelines:

    a. Be aware of organizational protocol. Respect the chain of command, and you have a much better chance of getting results.

    b. Phrase your request carefully. Even when your motives are pure, your words can easily be misunderstood by overly sensitive managers, especially if they are territorial about *their* departments.

    c. Ask for suggestions. Rather than asking for specific information, make the other people feel involved; let them know you respect their opinions and give them a chance to express opinions.

    d. Be sensitive to time restraints. It will not always be possible for others to meet your deadline. Find out if their schedule will permit compliance, and then take any steps necessary to fit your request into their schedule.

    e. Be aware of resource problems. If the other department is understaffed, your request might represent one more problem on a large pile of unfinished work. Offer help from your own department if that's practical.

    f. Apply meeting standards. Whenever you talk to another manager, you are holding a meeting, and the same rules for definition, assignment, and deadline apply.

    g. Follow up with a memo. Once someone else agrees to help, be sure that there are no misunderstandings about the work or the deadline.

3. When you complete assignments ahead of schedule, remember these rules:

    a. Don't change your style. Fast response is a positive trait, and it improves your reputation, even when you're criticized for coming through too quickly.

b. Hold off until the deadline. If you think a too-fast response will be perceived in a negative way, wait until the deadline.

c. Question criticism. Don't let it go by when someone tells you your response is too fast. Insist on more information. Once you eliminate inaccuracy, obvious errors, and incomplete work, the complaint has no valid basis.

d. Make fast response a positive trait. You will be seen as the person to come to when the pressure is on. As long as your reports and other assignments are done in a professional manner, others will respect your work.

e. Ensure high quality. If you plan to continue submitting work quickly, you must avoid the reputation of a person who does not also take great care, and become known for speed as well as for quality.

CHAPTER 11

1. Debate is a necessary phase in defining the problem to be addressed and often shows the way to the best solution. But debates can also represent political power struggles in the company. Apply these five rules for participating in a debate:

a. Accept discussion as a requirement. A debate is not necessarily a waste of time. In fact, it could be the most productive event during the meeting.

b. Point out differences of opinion. When a discussion seems to be going nowhere, chances are the two sides have not yet acknowledged that there may be two or more ideas about what the problem is. Raise this point and you will add clarity to the meeting.

c. Raise opposing points of view. When you present a case, bring up what others say in disagreement. Then explain why those points of view are flawed, or verbalize the points on which you agree.

d. Begin arguments with a premise. You will communicate your case more effectively if you first explain your perception of the problem. This will enlighten other attendees and might even bring up an important point: that others in the meeting have assumed a vastly different problem.

  e. Recognize motives. Be keenly aware that a discussion does not always center on the agenda issue. It might involve a power struggle between two or more managers or executives.

2. Negative meetings can be a great waste of time, because a stated agenda never gets achieved. Apply these guidelines:

  a. Be aware of the meeting's purpose. You will discover this purpose soon after the meeting begins. It might not involve an agenda at all. You will be best able to determine how to participate (or to remain silent) once you figure out what's really going on.

  b. Achieve results outside of the meeting. Don't try to apply positive guidelines during a negative meeting; it's a waste of time. Seek a different forum for achievement, preferably getting together with one other person or with smaller groups.

  c. Do not become involved. Stay out of the power struggles, and concentrate on your career, departmental, and personal goals. Getting involved in negative politics will make you part of the problem; refusing to play the game, ultimately, is the only solution to the problem.

  d. Maintain a neutral position. Don't let others classify you in one camp or another during an internal power struggle.

  e. Complain only through channels. In the most negative meeting situation, you might feel compelled to file a complaint. Go through your supervisor, and use the chain of command. Complaining to people who cannot or will not take any action in response is not going to solve the problem.

3. Being absolutely and completely truthful does not work in a meeting environment. There are appropriate times to speak out. Follow these standards:

  a. Think before you speak. Be aware of who is present, and when in doubt, wait for a more appropriate moment to make your statement.

  b. Phrase your arguments carefully. Be very aware of the words you use, especially when observing a flaw in someone else's style.

  c. Avoid speaking in absolutes. Leave room for discussion, and try not to close the door to discussion.

d. Present fact over opinion. If you merely tell others what you think, they will be unlikely to accept your views—especially when your opinion goes against popular ideas. Be prepared to back up your dissenting view with facts.

e. Show respect for common beliefs. Don't dismiss what others believe because they will resent your observations. Respect even the most obviously wrong idea, and offer alternatives cautiously.

f. Don't disagree just to make a point. Those who dissent just to convince others that they have a free mind become irritants in the meeting culture. The manager who occasionally makes a valid but opposing comment will receive more attention and respect from others.

g. Keep an open mind. The majority might just be right. When you present an opposing point of view, the response might be an explanation of why the popular view is valid. If you are mistaken, be willing to back down from your position.

CHAPTER 12

1. As an attendee, bringing up the problem someone else has in leading a meeting requires tact and concentration on the problem rather than on the person:

a. Define the problem in positive terms: To complain about a problem is never constructive, and it never leads to solutions. But offering a solution makes all the difference. It will improve the meeting by doing away with the problem, without involving a less productive series of complaints.

b. Remove the personality issue: Avoid saying that an individual is the problem, and put your energy into addressing and confronting issues. This keeps the discussion away from assigning blame.

c. Accept responsibility: If you accept the belief that there's nothing you can do, then you allow the problem to go unchanged. But if you take responsibility for improving the meetings you attend, then you can also create the solution needed.

d. Seek solutions by asking questions: The group and its leader will more willingly take part in developing answers when the solution is not imposed. Don't merely state the solution as you perceive it; define the problem by asking others for ideas.

e. Involve the meeting leader: Don't overlook the person running the meeting. Given the opportunity, the leader has a better chance for improving a poor condition than anyone else does.

2. The bureaucracy is difficult to take apart or bring down in size, because it exists to protect itself. And chances are that the bureaucratic approach is where the power rests in your company. When that is the case, you must work outside of the system. However, this creates new problems:

a. Creation of a larger bureaucracy: Many people have been frustrated in their efforts to reduce the bureaucracy, and they end up expanding it. Make sure your separate meetings are productive, simple, and get results. Otherwise, your attempts will only make the problem worse.

b. Power threats: Whenever someone takes action or tries to improve a situation, others will resist the change. People in positions of power—even when nothing is getting done—often feel threatened by effective action. You must always defend your position by pointing to results and never by justifying your sincerely well-motivated actions.

c. Approval: You must include your immediate supervisor in the decision to create your own series of meetings. If you cannot obtain approval, there's not much you can do to proceed. If you want to invite people from other departments, the approval question is made even more complex. The need to have a meeting is not always sufficient to grant the right; you must be able to function within the power structure in your company.

Index